MY
PRESCHOOLER

Other Books in the Minirth Meier New Life Clinic Series

For general information about Minirth Meier New Life Clinic branch offices, counseling services, educational resources, and hospital programs, call toll-free 1–800-NEW-LIFE.

MY PRESCHOOLER

READY
FOR NEW
ADVENTURES

Dr. Paul Warren

A JANET THOMA BOOK

THOMAS NELSON PUBLISHERS
Nashville • Atlanta • London • Vancouver

Copyright © 1994 by Dr. Paul Warren.

Published in Nashville, Tennessee, by Thomas Nelson, Inc., Publishers, and distributed in Canada by Word Communications, Ltd., Richmond, British Columbia.

The Bible version used in this publication is THE NEW KING JAMES VERSION. Copyright © 1979, 1980, 1982, 1990 Thomas Nelson, Inc., Publishers.

Anecdotes and case histories included in this volume are either hypothetical examples or composites of actual cases with names and details changed to protect identities.

Library of Congress Cataloging-in-Publication Data

Warren, Paul, 1949–
    My preschooler : ready for new adventures / Paul Warren.
        p.   cm. — (The Stepping-stones series for Christian parents)
    ISBN 0-7852-8346-3
    1. Preschool children.   2. Child rearing.   3. Parenting—Religious aspects—Christianity.   I. Title.   II. Series.
    HQ774.5.W37   1994
    649'.123—dc20   94–33800
                                                                          CIP

Printed in the United States of America.
1 2 3 4 5 6 — 99 98 97 96 95 94

To my wife, Vicky,
whose love of children
reminds me of God's love for children
and to my son, Matthew,
whose love teaches and encourages me.

CONTENTS

One laugh of a child
will make the holiest day more sacred still.

ROBERT INGERSOLL

ACKNOWLEDGMENTS

The author acknowledges the vision and direction of Janet Thoma, vice president of Thomas Nelson Publishers. Sandy Dengler's creativity made the manuscript come alive. Amy Glass's and Sue Ann Jones's careful editing kept the manuscript crisp and clear.

1. SNAPSHOTS OF LIFE

WINDOWS OF OPPORTUNITY

When all is done, human life is,
at the greatest and the best, but like a froward child,
that must be played with and humored a little
to keep it quiet till it falls asleep,
and then the care is over.

SIR WILLIAM TEMPLE, "Of Poetry"

A hundred flashes exploded as the band hit the first number at Fletcher High School's Christmas program. The scene on stage was worthy of those hundred pictures— a twinkling Christmas tree in the corner dressed in white bows, ten children in a still-life manger scene, each member of the band and choir dressed in formal holiday attire, and fake snow showering the entire ensemble. It was one of those picture-perfect moments.

Jennifer Lawton made sure she had a roll full of pictures of Sara, her two-year-old daughter. Sara played the part of the perfect angel as she knelt in front of the manger and folded her hands in prayer.

I've got to immortalize this moment, Jennifer thought. *This is probably the only time Sara's looked and acted like an angel.* Sara, at two-plus years old, was becoming quite the challenge for her single working mother.

Sharing the stage with Sara was Brian Jasper, also a two-year-old angel, who broke the proscenium to wave enthusiastically to Mommy and Daddy in the front row. The audience laughed and waved back.

Eight other tots completed the tableau.

Ten little children, sweet and eager and full of promise.

Assuming current social trends continue, thirty years from now, of those ten little pageant angels:

- One of the ten will either be dead or have been in jail.
- Five of the ten will be divorced.
- Two of the ten will suffer serious emotional dysfunction.
- Two of the ten will be in severe financial difficulty.
- One of the ten will be an alcoholic.

Not a cheery thought. None of the children or their parents will plan to have those problems. No actuarial overseer will arbitrarily dole out travail. What will have gone wrong?

The emotional and psychological development of those little stage door angels will largely determine who will see happiness and who will face the hangman. And the bulk of that development takes place in the first few years.

A Brief Moment in Time

The parents of angelic little Brian and Sara and their eight cohorts can take important steps now to ensure their children's success and happiness a decade from now. Those steps are neither onerous nor difficult. They are necessary.

The first three years of a child's life are foundational in the deepest sense. It is during this early part of life that basic biological, social, and psychological foundations are laid upon which every other childhood and adult experience will be based.

Brief snapshots of time. If certain needs are not addressed during these brief windows of opportunity, when necessary lessons "take" quickly and well, the child's emotional and psychological needs cannot easily be met later. If those needs are not met when they are supposed to be filled, that lack carries over into the next year of life and the next, the problems multiplying upon themselves. Thus, these windows of opportunity are moments to be captured . . . or else.

To illustrate, imagine that a group gathers at the top of a hill overlooking the Pacific Ocean, each person festooned with an assortment of sophisticated photographic equipment. The onlookers peer intently at a variable layer of clouds covering an ominously darkening sky. Most have traveled thousands of miles to observe this once-in-a-decade cosmic spectacle—a total solar eclipse.

"Two minutes to totality and counting," calls a fellow who has designated himself timekeeper.

The clouds, it would appear, are going to block out the event. The solar disk is nothing more than a bright smudge, hardly the thing of which *National Geographic* photos are made. Once past, the moment of totality will not return. Now or ever.

". . . Now!"

Just when hope seems bleakest, the cloud cover parts except for an insignificant haze. A narrow shaft of light hangs for a moment and melts to nothing as the black ball of the moon slips fully into place in front of the midday sun. Totality. A glowing ring around a black bull's-eye. The sky turns nighttime dark. Chills run through the onlookers, and it isn't air temperature that's causing them. Primal urges, primal mysteries, are at work here. Lose the sun at midday? Haunting. Frightening, even when you know the reason why. In a roadside ditch nearby, a confused chorus of dusk-singing tree frogs begins a tentative overture to the awesome mystery of the universe.

Brief moments later, another shaft of sun bursts out, and the event is over. Swiftly, it seems, the solar disk begins its arduous task of slipping free.

Little wonder that people wait years and spend thousands of dollars for this momentary experience. And it all happens within a very brief window of time.

A child's life can be compared to the window of opportunity an eclipse-watcher chases. Within a child's life there are brief snapshots of time where parents must seize certain opportunities to help him or her. If that parental support has not occurred, the child will be able to make up the loss only with great difficulty, if at all. Moreover, this third season of life, beyond toddlerhood but before nursery school, is the last real opportunity for achieving some of the tasks the child must complete. It is now or never.

The Other Development

This book will not cover ground already covered competently by many other writers. A number of excellent works are available that deal with the physical aspects of a toddler's growth such as how to respond when fever strikes and what growth criteria are normal for two-year-olds.

Instead, I would like to concentrate on the aspects of a child's development the other books do not emphasize or perhaps fail to mention—the child's psychological, emotional, social, and spiritual development. When the needs pertaining to this development are attended to, health and happiness bloom.

There's a lot a parent can do to further the child's growth in these areas. There are also parental behaviors to avoid and attitudes to change; I will discuss those issues as well.

Development to This Point

Tom Jasper carried his two-year-old Brian out the auditorium door on his shoulder. Brian's head pressed against his neck and the limp little arm flopped in rhythm with his walking.

Beside him, Marsha grinned. "Sound asleep."

"Yeah." Tom handed the keys to Marsha so she could open the back door of the car. "This kid has two modes only: sleep and noise."

That just about summarizes the preschool age. To an adult, the child seems to either sleep or bounce off the walls, babble incessant nonsense, do stupid stuff, deliberately annoy, and get into everything. Believe it or not, however, none of those wild childish behaviors is random or purposeless. In these brief years, a period in which people used to think nothing significant happened in the child's development, the child's philosophy, emotions, attitudes, and strategies are being forged for a lifetime. At the beginning of this momentous time, the child's personality will not yet be clearly shaped. By its close, the child will be pretty much what he or she will always be.

In this book we will look at the specific opportunities that are best exploited within those brief windows of opportunity during the preschool parade of changes. Of course some concerns, such as language development and discipline, are general and continue throughout the child's life. However, the way a parent best capitalizes upon the windows of opportunity affecting language and discipline depends markedly upon the child's age. So in this book

I'll provide suggestions for how you can have the most positive impact on language and development—and other issues—during your child's preschool years.

No child is the same two days in a row; capabilities and perceptions change as rapidly as size does. Parents must exploit these changes, understanding that what worked yesterday may not work today. Tomorrow brings its own uniqueness.

There are essentially six major opportunities during the first three seasons of life (infancy, toddlerhood, and preschool). Before we launch into the preschool needs related to those opportunities, let's review what your child needed during the first two stages of his or her life.

The First Year of Life

Tom Jasper described his newborn Brian as "a blob," and he wasn't far from wrong. The tiny creature seemed to sleep and eat, for the most part. Their pediatrician carefully monitored Brian's physical growth, which occurred rapidly, but it did not appear that anything else was happening. That appearance was false, however. The newborn boy was already blotting up any number of messages about the world.

During the first year of life, a major responsibility is to solidify the relationship between child and parent. How successfully this is done influences the pattern of relationships this child will have throughout the rest of his or her life. To do this, you, as a parent, are given two specific opportunities to aid your infant.

1. Enabling Your Child to Trust. An infant's first and most lasting lesson in trust comes during this year. By trust I mean the solid, bone-deep confidence that other human beings will come through and fulfill the infant's needs. A child learns this from consistent loving attention by a primary caregiver. Parents teach this trust by responding promptly to their baby's cries and fulfilling the baby's needs promptly, or nearly so. Way down below verbal level, these simple, repetitious acts tell a child, "We are here for you. You can depend upon other people."

2. Helping Your Child Cope with the Fear of Abandonment. Abandonment is an infant's first and deepest fear. And why not? The baby is totally at the mercy of others. The attention, nurturing, and care he or she receives from others is fully voluntary on their part. The baby has no clout, no means of coercion. How do you teach a child who lacks both verbal capability and the ability to understand abstractly, *They will not forsake me?*

Silly games like peek-a-boo bore parents to death but they teach a child, below conscious level, that out of sight does not mean abandonment. The face behind the newspaper leaves. It comes back. It leaves. It comes back. Even better, the process is pleasant. Fun.

Parents also impart this subtle lesson when they leave the baby for brief periods with another caring adult and then return in a timely manner. Again the baby perceives the message, *I leave. I return. I'll not forsake you.*

A note of clarification is appropriate here. I am not implying that an infant's best interest is ever served by a day care situation, particularly one extending more than a few hours during the waking day. Day care before one year teaches just the opposite lesson the infant needs—you can't trust Mommy or Daddy to be there. You see, to an infant, a minute is as big as an hour. The child has no time reference, no sense of measured time passing.

What makes extended absences damaging when the same absence would scarcely ruffle the feathers of an eighteen-month-old is the infant's unique status of possessing no personal identity yet. An infant *is* the parents in every sense of the word: a mathematical identity, an extension of the caregiver. That status will begin to change by the end of the first year, and by the close of the second year the child will be very much his or her own person. But now, during these first months, the child's sense of trust and security depends upon an intimate and almost constant association with the caregiver.

The Second Year

"What a year! 'Terrible twos' is right!" Jenny Lawton stared glassy-eyed at her Sara's baby book.

"From about eighteen months 'til two and a half, Brian was all boy. But he's mellowed out some now," Marsha Jasper assayed. "I wouldn't say 'terrible,' exactly. But challenging."

I never say "terrible." A wonderful and mystical transformation takes place during this age. The child discovers *Self.* He or she realizes, *I am a person separate from others. I have my needs and desires, and other people have needs and desires that are not necessarily mine. I still strongly suspect I am the center of the universe, but there are occasionally reasons to doubt it.*

The child establishes an identity separate from the parents' identities in two ways: by making choices (a mere adjunct of a parent would be unable to make separate choices) and by contesting the parent's authority. This is not rebellion in the classic sense. Rebellion hopes for a different outcome. This does not. The child knows the parent is bigger, stronger, quicker, smarter. By challenging the parents, the child does not say, "I want changes around here," but rather, "I am an individual separate from you. See? I have chosen a different way to go." The challenge itself is the statement, not the hoped-for outcome.

Parents must maintain and improve the parent-child relationship with their toddler while simultaneously helping the child establish a personal identity apart from the parents. Two additional opportunities aid in this.

1. Allow Your Child Narcissistic Wounding Experiences. Narcissistic wounding is a term for those experiences where a child learns he or she is no longer the center of the universe. Mommy has needs. Daddy does, too, and maybe an older sister or brother as well. The toddler begins to understand the world was not created to gratify him or her.

A child is usually not mature enough to grasp this concept until about eighteen months of age. From this point on, a parent must gradually introduce situations where this child learns to wait or is denied what he or she wants. If narcissistic wounding doesn't occur at this age, the child grows into an entitled creature (in other words, a spoiled brat).

2. Help Your Child Experiment with the Teeter-Totter of Independence/Dependence. The toddler who does not exhibit some form of independence and opposition offers reason for concern. Experimentation with small incidents of independence and self-control are absolutely essential if a child is to be successful at establishing a strong self-identity.

For example, little Sara engaged in a food fight with her grandmother—not throwing food at each other, of course, but making it a control issue. Grandma tried to get her to eat. She refused. Grandma insisted. Sara persisted. In so doing, Sara established herself as a person apart from her primary caregiver, her grandmother.

Little Brian was not so obvious. When he crawled into his daddy's lap to read a book he insisted on holding it and turning the pages himself. Sometimes he didn't wait until the text was completed; sometimes he lingered. He was marching to his own drummer, a beat he was hearing for the very first time.

The parent who becomes a partner with the child in this great leap of separation and individuation will probably have far less trouble than would someone like Sara's grandma, who is locked in a power struggle. Here are some things a parent might do to ease this transition:

- *Be available to provide encouragement after failure and praise after success.* Most importantly, measure that failure and success according to two-year-old standards, not by adult or big-kid guidelines.

- *Surrender some control and let the child take risks.* We're not talking about playing with plastic dry-cleaning bags and running in the streets, of course. Not genuine safety hazards but little hazards, allowed within reason. Apply this acid test: "If my child tries that, is real harm likely?" Unless the answer is a firm yes, provide a little latitude. An overly controlled environment impedes a child's experiments in individuality. A carefully planned and childproofed home environment can encourage it.

- *Save the absolute* no *for situations in which it is necessary.* These situations include wrongdoing (theft, for example), safety hazards (riding in the car without a safety restraint), and occasions where a child would seriously injure an animal, annoy persons, or damage someone's property.

During this second year, one other phenomenon bears greatly upon the third year—integration. Infants and children just past their first birthday see everything as all good or all bad. Mommy is either all lovable (doing something nice, gratifying the child) or all nasty (refusing to permit some desired action or treat). About the eighteen-month milestone, give or take a few weeks or months, the child grasps the reality that people can be both good and bad (rated subjectively, of course). Once that realization takes place, the child takes the next logical step, realizing, *I am integrated as well, neither all good nor all bad.*

If all these lessons of the first two seasons proceed fairly well (Perfection is not essential—would that we could achieve it!), a solid foundation is laid for this season. The mechanics of independence—of Self—should be in place. The child who has not successfully dealt with the teeter-totter of independence/dependence in the prior year will either be a "hell-on-wheels" trying to establish that independence or a "clinging vine" who's terrified of the outside world and of new experiences. Sometimes the same child will be both, depending upon the situation as the child perceives it.

If behavior of that sort leads you to suspect that your child has not yet mastered the skills of the first two years, I recommend the second book in this series, *My Toddler: The Beginning of Independence,* which can help you understand in greater detail what the first two seasons of a child's life require.

For now, though, let's assume you and your child have

pretty much capitalized upon the opportunities to date. You are both ready for the third season of life, by many measures, perhaps, the most exciting.

Well . . . as ready as you'll ever be.

To begin, let's look at some parenting strategies that will work well during the year from your child's second birthday to the third, helping him or her grow emotionally and psychologically in healthy ways.

2. LEARNING WHAT WORKS

EFFECTIVE PARENTING

Time is that wherein there is opportunity,
and opportunity is that wherein
there is no great time.

HIPPOCRATES, *Precepts*

J ennifer Lawton, first-time mother, was learning a whole lot about parenting in an awful hurry . . . not that she got to do all that much of it. Following high school graduation she'd gone to work full time at a fast-food restaurant, grilling burgers. During all her school and work hours, her own mom took care of little Sara.

Tonight, following the Christmas program, Jenny lifted her temporarily angelic Sara off the stage. "What a good job you did!" she cooed. "You were so quiet and pretty."

"Down. Me down!" Sara yelled. She kicked, nailing Jenny hard enough to arouse suspicion that it was no accident.

"Sara!" She put Sara on the floor. Sara scooted off, burrowing into the throng of departing audience members. "Sara! Sara, come back here!" Jenny shouldered her way through the lingering crowd, thinking how incredibly easy it is to hide yourself when you're two feet high.

"Lose something?" Bulky and baritone, Bob Charleston came toward Jenny, pushing through the milling people. As easily as Jenny would heft a hot dog he was carrying Sara, her head as high as his.

More than slightly embarrassed, Jenny took Sara out of his arms. "She needs a big iron anchor."

"My kids could make it into the next county before I could find my whip and chair." He grinned. "But then, I have boys—'active' boys, I think the euphemism is."

"Are they here?" Jenny recognized Bob from the single-parents class here at the church, but she'd never seen his children. She knew only that he had two.

"Yeah. The two shepherds with the fidgets. Your Sara was quieter than they were, although I didn't know then she was yours. You'd think grade-schoolers could stand still a minute."

"Hey, you saw all the standing still Sara has ever done in her whole life, right up there. At least she did it for the pageant. I'm really proud of her. And I don't blame her for uncorking and running afterward. She's just one of those kids; it's awfully hard for her to be still." She smiled, feeling like a first-class goof. "Sorry. You know, I didn't realize you'd be here. Shame on me, but I don't remember you at any of the practices."

"No shame on you. The boys' baby-sitter brought them. She's the reason they're in this pageant—her husband is the band director."

"Oh." That figured. Jennifer surely would have noticed Bob. He was really noticeable with that rugged, tanned face and the acre of teeth that gleamed when he smiled. "Well, uh, it's nice to see you here. And your shepherds did okay."

"Thanks. I'll tell them that; tell them it's from a woman who really knows her shepherds."

Jennifer felt herself blushing. She hated when she blushed! And always at the wrong time. "Thanks for retrieving my kid. I appreciate it."

"Happy to. Merry Christmas."

"Yeah. I mean, merry Christmas to you too." Jenny was being a complete dolt. She acted like she was still in junior high.

Two little shepherds called lustily to Bob. He and Jenny swapped hasty good-byes, then he disappeared toward the stage.

Jenny's mom appeared from nowhere by her side. "Now who is that? Is that someone we know?"

"I don't think so. He goes to the early service, I think."

Sara squirmed to be let down. Jenny hung on. Sara squirmed harder and started kicking. Why did she always behave her worst when her grandma was watching?

Jenny's mom smiled one of those grim smiles of hers that contained no mirth whatsoever. "I want to introduce you and Sara to Hazel Singleton—you remember your father and me talking about the Singletons back in Memphis. It will only take a few minutes. Do you suppose," she asked with her maddening phony sweetness, "that you could make Sara behave like a civilized person for just a few minutes?"

"What a sweet little angel," a woman cooed, ruffling Sara's hair as the little one streaked by her.

Jenny's mom muttered, "If she only knew."

The Role Your Parents Played

Because of her situation, Jenny found herself in constant contact—and at constant odds—with her own mother's parenting attitudes and techniques. But all of us parents are strongly influenced by our own parents' parenting, even if we aren't in immediate contact with them.

Human beings are not only the sum of their past experiences; they also tend to repeat the familiar. Unless parents deliberately set out to change things, they will probably be the same kind of parents their own parents were, even if their childhood experience was painful. This is one reason why children who were abused grow up to become parents who abuse. Certainly they know how much it hurts. And yet, they end up hurting their children.

Parents may also intentionally adopt a parenting philosophy that is diametrically opposed to their own parents' philosophy. In other words, their parents' attitudes and techniques still strongly influence them but in a way that invites rebellion rather than repetition.

Many people—usually people with a stable, happy childhood—examine their parents' methods and adjust them for personal fit. Perhaps they'll deliberately be more lenient in this area, less lenient in that. Perhaps they'll crack down in some regard that their parents did not. That's logical and good. The times our children live in are not the same as the times we grew up in.

Analyze the Influences in Your Past

When parents come to me for counseling (more properly, for counseling their children), they've usually spent the last ten years playing firefighter. A fire erupts here, so they put it out. One flares up over there, and they stomp it out, too, hoping it doesn't spread. But too often it *does* spread. I see firefighting a lot. The parent sees a potential trouble spot or misbehavior and tries to stop it. Then the parent sees another problem area and tries to correct it. In all this there is no view of the whole, no strategy, no awareness of a goal.

When those parents come, we address the problem by analyzing their present techniques, looking for differences that will make their parenting more effective, framing an overall strategy of parenting, and setting a goal. You can benefit from just this same approach.

Begin with analysis. First, identify your parents' methods and strategy. Then compare the similarities and differences between your parents' methods and your own. As a third step, analyze what is effective in your situation and what methods simply don't work.

This is important information for the parents of a preschooler because a walking, talking child is starting to require the same methods of discipline that older children need. There will have to be important changes in technique as the child grows, but the basics begin now.

You can analyze your attitudes and techniques too. To start, plumb your memories for an early incident in your life in which your parents engaged in some strong interaction with you. It could be a loving occasion with happy memories or an incident involving harsh discipline or a time when their priorities clashed with yours. Parenting is not just disciplining. It also involves praise, nurturing, protection, guidance, and loving acts such as comforting, hugging, and reassuring.

Describe the incident in which you had some strong interaction with your parents.

_____

_____

_____

_____

What was your mother's reaction?

_____

_____

_____

_____

What was your father's reaction?

_____

_____

_____

_____

What were your feelings at the time?

_____

_____

_____

_____

Have your feelings changed? If so, how?

_____

_____

_____

_____

Survey your memories for other notable or vivid incidents. They need not be important in the classic sense of life-changing. Actually, they were life-changing—all well-remembered incidents are—but they may seem minor. That's all right.

Keep in mind that the purpose of this exercise is never to lay any sort of blame on your parents (and that includes condoned blame, such as "He didn't mean to" or "She didn't know"). Rather, you simply want to see what their influences are and how much you want those influences to guide you in your own parenting. There is no right and wrong, particularly because your child is unique and requires a unique touch, just as you are unique.

Now, using the list below, analyze your mother's and father's strategies separately. Identify with an *M* those traits your mother commonly exhibited—for instance, most of the time she did this. Mark your father's commonly expressed traits with an *F.* Traits and methods your parents shared might be identified with *MF.* Recognize that neither your mother nor your father had to present a particular trait 100 percent of the time for it to qualify. Many of the traits below will not be marked at all.

_____ a. Was cool and distant, standoffish.

_____ b. Was warm and affectionate, lots of physical contact.

_____ c. Was physically abusive with frequent hitting or slapping.

_____ d. Rarely or never employed corporal punishment.

_____ e. Used corporal punishment with restraint.

_____ f. Was emotionally abusive, yelling, belittling, denigrating.

_____ g. Was good at praising and positive reinforcement.

_____ h. Employed frequent bribes to enforce behavior.

_____ i. Was controlling, perhaps strongly controlling, allowing no deviation from what that parent thought was the way to do something.

_____ j. Was very wishy-washy, with little clear guidance or control, rarely "put his or her foot down."

_____ k. Had a firm opinion of what constituted good behavior and bad behavior. Strongly moral, ethical (or immoral, unethical).

_____ l. Seemed to understand how kids think at various ages.

_____ m. Drew one line for behavior and that was it, regardless of age.

_____ n. Corrected, warned, and threatened punishment, but hardly ever followed through. You could get away with murder.

_____ o. Discipline was erratic and unpredictable. Behavior that was okay one time, or tolerated at least, was punished the next time.

_____ p. Parent had (or still has) emotional, psychological, or physical problems that adversely affected parenting.

_____ q. Parent strongly favored one sibling over another.

1. Analyzing for Consistency. How many of the traits above did you mark with an *M* and an *F?* If your parents shared a third to half of all the traits marked, even if some of the marked traits were negatives, they exhibited remarkable consistency between themselves. They agreed on procedures even if you might not have liked those procedures.

The other form of consistency that is important is represented by the trait described in statement *o.* When parents punish a child for a specific behavior one time then let it pass the next, that's serious inconsistency. Actually, such inconsistency is easy to slip into. The parent may simply be too tired or drained from a demanding day to care enough to respond. "The kid's killing the cat? Let him. I'm past caring. I'm done for the day."

2. *Analyzing for Effectiveness.* Go through the traits you identified in your mother. Think about your reactions and responses. Did her methods work well? Okay usually? Not at all? What was effective? What was not? What would have worked better?

Do the same with those traits you identified in your father. How effective were the methods your father employed?

Did your parents' methods work better or worse on your siblings? You and your siblings are very different. What personality types responded well to which traits?

Analyzing Your
Parenting Techniques

We'll analyze your parenting techniques three ways. The first way, in particular, will require an honest appraisal of yourself. You can easily lie to yourself, fudge a little, and feel better. Don't. Be harshly truthful with yourself as you answer the questions below.

First, I asked you earlier to describe an incident from early in your life in which your parents had some strong interaction with you. Now describe how you, as a parent, would have responded if that incident had taken place in your child's life.

_____

_____

_____

_____

For the second way we'll analyze your parenting, describe a memorable parenting encounter in your child's life, something that happened since the child started walking and talking.

_____

_____

_____

_____

What was your reaction?

_____

_____

_____

_____

What was your spouse's reaction?

_____

_____

_____

_____

What were your feelings at the time you were engaged in the incident?

_____

_____

_____

_____

_____

Have your feelings changed? If so, how?

_____

_____

_____

_____

_____

Third, pick a few more occasions when you were deeply involved in some nurturing, disciplining instance with your child. Based on these incidents you're thinking about, rate yourself on the list of traits you marked with *M*s and *F*s on pages 23–24. Mark an *I* next to the traits that apply to you. Try not to mark what you *wish* were so; instead, mark what your techniques actually are based upon the incidents analyzed here.

Did you mark many traits that also have an *M* or *F*?

Every person is unique, and so is every person's parenting methods. I cannot say "this is good" and "that is not" (except for certain traits such as abusiveness, which are unequivocally wrong) in your case. No one but you can.

But as you think about this exercise, you should be able to see to what degree your parents' methods are influencing you. You should be able to grasp whether your methods are effective now and whether they are going to be effective as your child gets older.

You should also see how well your methods agree with your spouse's methods. They should be consistent—the more consistent the better. In fact, even when the trait is undesirable, such as when one person is strongly authoritarian and the other abrogates authority altogether, it is better that both parents employ the same strategies. It does more damage than good when one tries to balance the spouse's extreme by going to the opposite extreme. Let me tell you the story of one of the other little angels in that pageant, Anna.

When she was almost four, Anna was talking with the maturity of a ten-year-old. As bright as she was articulate, she stormed through life certain that what she wanted should always prevail. She was not spoiled in the classic sense. She did not expect the world to dump its goodies lavishly upon her. However, at almost four she did expect the world to follow where she led.

Her mother had always wanted a little girl, but what the mother actually wanted was, well, a doll. An obedient early-Shirley Temple clone to dress in frills and show off to the world. What she got was a tornado in overalls who elevated screaming to an art. Her daddy hadn't wanted a girl at all. He wanted a son to follow him around and help wax the car and appreciate baseball.

Anna fit Daddy's dream closer than Mommy's. Mommy sternly and consistently tried to shape Anna into a proper little girl by constantly correcting what she perceived to be unladylike behavior. Dual screaming matches were commonplace. Mommy assumed some sort of equilibrium would eventually be reached in which the yelling would cease—presumably, when Anna finally knuckled under. Daddy, on the other hand, was a marshmallow. The more Mommy imposed strictness, the more lenient he became. Already Anna was skilled at manipulating her parents, pitting one against the other, wheedling, and "getting away with murder."

Some Things That Work, Some That Don't

Effectiveness. That's the bottom line. Why engage in some pursuit if it's bound to accomplish nothing? Daddy was way ahead of Mommy when it came to Rule Number One, the foremost parenting guideline:

1. Relationships Come First
Mommy prided herself as a mother, but in fact she was not being a mother at all. She was a behavior cop.

She did not know her child well on a personal basis, and there was no indication that she would do so in the future. Daddy fared better. When Daddy went out for a load of firewood for the fireplace, he took Anna along. Down to the mini mart for milk? Sure, Honey, come along. Anna babbled constantly, and Daddy didn't turn her off. The sun rose and set on her daddy.

Now, in these first few years, is the time when you should be building a lifelong relationship with your child. This runs against the grain with a lot of fathers. Many men tend to let Mom raise the kid to an age that's more fun. When the child can go to sporting events, go hunting or fishing, go to the amusement park—that's when Dad starts to take an interest in being a dad. That's usually ten years too late.

The relationship is built by spending affection and time. There is no shortcut. Daddy did not play games with Anna. He did not read to her, although that is the best way by far to build relationships. But he included her, snuggled her when she needed snuggling, laughed with her, talked to her, let her talk. He let her be part of his personal life.

A healthy child begins by being totally identified with the parent and then separates step by step throughout childhood. By the age of twelve, the child stands apart from Mom and Dad literally and figuratively. That is the final stage of separation—the time when relationships change, not when they can begin. Relationships begin at the beginning—now, with the small child.

2. Control What You Can Control, and Don't Try to Control What You Cannot

You can control very nearly every aspect of a small child's life because the child is still so intimately associated with you. You and the household are virtually the child's whole world. Still, you cannot control the child's feelings.

"Don't you dare be mad at Mommy!" is an ineffective and damaging statement. Compare it with "Don't you dare behave that way toward Mommy!" See the difference? You can regulate behavior. You cannot regulate feelings. Don't try.

As your child grows, you will control less and less of his or her behavior and existence. Recognize that limitation.

For example, a woman we'll call Winona strongly suspected that her twelve-year-old son had taken up smoking. To catch him, she would search his room while he was in school. Winona's snooping did nothing but alienate the boy. He wised up almost instantly to her searches and didn't bring home anything to trigger suspicion. He did, however, stash little traps now and then, just for kicks. In his underwear drawer he hid a dried, squashed toad he peeled off the street, knowing she'd find it, knowing she couldn't say anything without revealing her searches, knowing she'd bust keeping her mouth shut. When he set a mousetrap in his sneaker she knew he was on to her, but that didn't stop her. She was bent on controlling something she could not control.

A more effective course? Winona could safely say, "You will not smoke in my house or in my presence, and these are the reasons why I disapprove of your smoking at all." That was not only enforceable, it gave her son guidance and the reasons behind the guidance.

3. Consider the Child

The limitations of the child's age, tendencies, and temperament should all shape your approach to parenting.

Here is where Jenny shone as a mother. She understood that Sara was a naturally overactive child. She praised Sara's fine job as an angel and understood Sara's need to blow off steam afterward. She praised immediately, while the deed was fresh. Her mom never caught on to Sara's uniqueness. Jenny's mom treated Sara's over-activity as a perverse example of being naughty. Note also that Jenny's mom failed to praise Sara's good behavior during the pageant—indeed, it would appear she either failed to notice it or took it for granted.

Winona was treating her son like a three-year-old. She was not taking into consideration that the boy was within five years of virtual adulthood. Snooping is totally appropriate for the parent of a preschooler, perhaps even a grade-schooler. But by the time the child reaches twelve, he or she should be enjoying most of the privileges of adulthood, privacy among them.

A one- or two-year-old is not capable of self-discipline. The preschooler may be headed down the road in the right direction, but he or she is not yet capable of consistent self-control. You must take that into consideration. We will deal at length with discipline for this age later in a section of its own.

4. Be Consistent

Anna's parents were plunging headlong down a dead end. They were violating the two-part consistency rule. Consistency takes two forms: One is consistency within each parent. If Mommy has laid down a law of life, she is to enforce that law consistently. She cannot be too tired to care now and then, and she cannot let the child routinely talk her out of it. (Certainly there can be exceptions, however. I am not advocating blind rigidity.)

Also, Mommy and Daddy must remain consistent

with each other. They must support the same agenda by similar means. Anna's parents didn't do that. Mommy clamped down; Daddy let up. Daddy let it be known it was okay to do such-and-so, but don't let Mommy catch you.

You can build consistency in your own parenting in several ways. First, go through the list of traits *a* through *q* on pages 23–24 with your spouse. Agree between yourselves what traits you want to use for this particular child. Don't just do it once forever. Repeat the process frequently enough that you both remain on the same wavelength.

Also, make certain you are being consistent yourself. If something is naughty on one occasion, it's naughty—not cute when done in private. Too tired to enforce a rule? Bestir yourself. It's worth it in the long run.

5. Keep the Goal in Mind

The purpose of parenting is to send the child out into the world independent and yet capable of both attachment—that is, solid interpersonal relationships—and self-control. Ideally, the child will have a conscience that guides him or her well without generating excessive guilt.

That is the goal. If parenting is unerringly directed toward that goal, parenting will be effective. What will help the child know right from wrong? I mean, true right from true wrong, not some idiosyncrasy of the parents such as "I don't like that kind of hairstyle. That's wrong."

Jenny's mom, bless her, was not the least hard-hearted. She loved her grandchild and wanted what was best for Sara. But she also wanted a quiet child. She assumed, because her generation was taught to assume, that Sara was a clean slate to be written upon and shaped however Grandma wanted to shape her. She hoped that browbeating Sara at an early age would achieve the proper shaping. She operated from pure motives, but that did not automatically make her methods effective.

The parents of little preschool angels would do well to pause and reflect from time to time (not when weary and not in the heat of anger, but during reflective times) on these questions: Will this strategy on my part help the child learn self-control? Does my child see solid relationships in myself and in others so he or she can learn by observing? Is my relationship with my child a close and affectionate one? What practical things can I do to improve matters? Does my child know I am operating in his or her best interests?

Explanations do not work well on a two-year-old for a number of reasons. Preschoolers, though, are starting to understand that there are whys and wherefores, and they can grasp those explanations to an extent. To how great an extent depends upon the child. Some kids pick up on cause and effect quite early; others never do seem to grasp it well.

Adjusted to the child's growth and development, these precepts are the foundation upon which you will later lay all the rest of your efforts.

3. I'M NOT A BABY ANYMORE

PHYSICAL DEVELOPMENT

You learn many things from children.
How much patience you have, for instance.

FRANKLIN P. JONES

Why discuss a preschooler's physical growth at all if this is a book on emotional and psychological development? Because emotional and psychological well-being depend upon physical well-being. Conversely, physical well-being depends upon emotional and psychological health. That's why.

Day care workers and nurses in public health clinics can tell immediately which of the toddlers and preschoolers they see come from stable homes and which are not receiving the nurturing they require. Children putting all their energy into surviving just do not grow and develop as well as well-nurtured children do.

A famous study on infant growth illustrates this. The subjects of the study were a group of infants observed over the course of a year. Some of them went from the hospital to homes where love and nurturing were in short supply. The babies were fed well enough; still, their physical growth suffered. These infants were then removed from their homes and put back in the hospital, where they were given round-the-clock care. The care included snuggling, face-to-face interaction, and other kinds of nurturing. The babies started to grow again. The researchers were actually able to turn the babies' physical growth off and on by turning off and on the close nurturing beyond feeding. Children's growth is that intricately tied to love—to emotional nurturing.

In this preschool period, your child's physical growth will slow as far as adding pounds and inches, but the child's shape will change dramatically. This shift from toddler to preschooler requires a great deal of energy. On top of that, the child is growing in important psychological and emotional ways as well. That takes energy also. The energy of physical growth, then, is shunted over to physical change.

Growing and Changing

"Curious," said Marsha Jasper just a little proudly. "Before we had Brian I liked babies. Now I see them from a whole new perspective. Sure, I still like them. Love them. But now I can look at a baby and tell you how old it is within a month or so. I don't know how I can do it, but I'm usually pretty close."

It's not just size, for there are petite babies and husky babies. Babies change so dramatically through the first two years that their degree of coordination and their proportions—the size of their head, arms, and legs compared with the size of their torso—give away their age quite accurately. Toddlers change more subtly, from clumsy, chunky babies just learning to walk to the leggy, sinewy young children in the third year of life. Not until the age of two can children clap their hands above their heads. Along with elongated body shape, their coordination and motor skills change just as dramatically. The preschooler is child-shaped, albeit in miniature. These changes are not particularly noticeable from day to day. But viewed in perspective, they are quantum leaps toward adulthood.

Motor Skills

Prior to nursery school, a child will become adept at most of the motor skills learned over the first two years, including walking, climbing, and running. In fact, that will be what constitutes play at this age—sheer activity.

This certainly was the case for Sara Lawton. Every time Sara's feet touched the ground she was off, not walking, but running everywhere she went. Jennifer found her on the kitchen countertop one time peering over the top of the refrigerator. Sara had pulled a chair over and climbed up on it to reach the counter.

Be careful about leaving anything like a ladder around. A preschooler will go right up the rungs. That's why climbing toys and swing sets are such a hit for kids this age.

Tricycles are another favorite toy. Mastering trike riding is a heady experience for your little one. Don't forget the helmet.

"Helmet?" you may ask. "For a *tricycle?*"

Helmets serve several important purposes at this age apart from protecting heads from falls. In fact, that's the least of it when a toddler mounts a trike. After all, it's not that far to the ground.

Many areas require by law that (two-wheel) cyclists wear helmets. I wish every place did. Thousands of head injuries causing permanent brain damage happen to bikers, and as often as not the biker was not at fault. If you introduce the habit of wearing a helmet the first time your youngster climbs on the trike, when he or she graduates to a two-wheeler, wearing a helmet will be as natural as working the pedals.

There is also a psychological value to that little foam helmet. Adults wear helmets when they ride. Big kids do too. That helmet, like a big shiny badge, says, *I am growing! I am big!* Below conscious level it also says, *I am important enough to protect.* These are all messages of encouragement that help the child grow emotionally and psychologically. They are nurturing.

Another physical change you'll notice in your child is in his or her weight and height.

Weight and Height Gain

"What gain?" asked Jenny.

"Of course she doesn't gain. Sara doesn't eat enough!" insisted Jenny's mom, and every meal became a battleground between an anxious grandma who wanted her granddaughter to *eat!* and an equally stubborn child who refused.

Actually, Sara was doing just fine, as evidenced by the extravagant amount of energy she burned up by running. During the second year, a child's physical growth screeches to a near halt. From now on it will continue at a measured pace. On the average, most children gain between four and five pounds over their entire third year. Contrast this with the first year of life, when the average infant gains from one-fourth to one-half pound per week.

This is not to suggest that gains are steady. Growth occurs in spurts. A child's physical growth will plateau out, only to take off again a few months later. This does not suggest that nothing happens during the plateau period. Internal growth and change are going on. It's just not easily quantifiable the way weight and height are.

Children will grow somewhere between three and five inches in height each of the next few years. Since checkups at the pediatrician's office are usually needed only once a year now, you can monitor your own child's growth at home if you wish. Size gain is not important, though. Emotional, psychological, and neurological (coordination, motor skills) gains are.

Children enjoy seeing visual proof of their growth, and not just at this age. The story comes to mind of a farm couple who raised their kids in a big, old-fashioned farmhouse during the thirties. They recorded the growth of all the kids on a wooden door frame. When the kids were grown and they sold the farm, they ripped out that framing board, all black with names and pencil-drawn lines, and took it with them to their new home. There was too much pride and history in that board to leave it behind.

Rather than tear your door apart, you might wish to make or purchase a simple growth chart to hang in your home. Most are made of felt, fabric, or poster board and are graduated in inches or have a measuring tape attached; they're usually decorated with some tall creature—a giraffe, Michael Jordan, whatever. If possible, make or buy one that measures to four or five feet in height.

You might choose to pencil in your child's height every birthday with periodic checks in between. If possible, make every member of the family a part of this growth chart. Measure your family members in their stocking feet, of course, or Mom would have an unfair advantage in three-inch spikes.

A friend found a very small child's rocking chair at a garage sale and used it as a photo point. Each child, on his or her birthday, was photographed in that little rocker. At age one her son knelt on the rocker seat facing backward with his hands gripping the back. At age two he sat in it the normal way and his feet just barely touched the floor. At the age of twelve, already the tallest kid on his church soccer team, he was photographed holding the chair in one hand. What a priceless record those twelve snapshots are!

If you don't notice at least some increase in your child's height during a six-month period, contact your pediatrician. Rarely, children cease growing due to a hormonal imbalance. It's treatable, but the sooner you catch this problem the better because most children cannot make up for lost growth once the imbalance occurs. Very, *very* rarely, kidney or other organ malfunction retards or halts growth. And lest you become alarmed, let me assure you that sometimes children's growth slows to near imperceptibility; it's still happening, but not enough to notice.

Changes in Proportion
Here's where all the energy is being used. Gone is the bowed back and protruding tummy. The stubby, chunky little arms and legs lengthen out into long, almost skinny appendages. That curious little fat fold halfway between wrist and elbow disappears.

Sara's grandma looked at the child's puny arms, sighed a heavy "Tsk-tsk," and redoubled her efforts to get Sara to eat. Her efforts were in vain. For one thing, food had become a control issue in their case. It was no longer a matter of nourishment but of "Who's the boss here?" (Sara was winning, hands down.) Sara's grandma's fears were also in vain. It's normal for a child of three or four to look skinny and fragile. It takes awhile for muscle mass to catch up with the changes in bone proportions. This was the case with Sara, who tended to be petite anyway.

Brian Jasper, on the other hand, was, to say the least, robust. Always was, always will be. He lost that crease in his forearm, but he never lost the chunkiness. Chunkiness is something to which parents ought to pay attention.

The Roots of Obesity

"Obese?" Brian's mom, Marsha, scoffed. "Husky, yes. Obese, hardly. He's a big boy; that's all."

She may well be right. Children and adults all vary widely based upon their genetic tendencies. But . . .

About the time obese children enter the first or second grade, they will become a target of ridicule. Grade-schoolers are very big into competitiveness and comparison. It's their new measure of life. Anyone out of the ordinary quickly gets noticed and commented upon. Being called "Fats" doesn't help one's self-esteem a bit, even if it's preceded by "Minnesota." By the time these children enter school, their eating and exercise habits are already well established, although certainly not yet set in cement. Obesity, as opposed to the genetic tendency to huskiness, begins to show up in children as they approach school age. At this stage, it is far, far easier to nip problems in the bud than to tackle them later, when long-term eating and exercise habits as well as self-esteem issues have become ingrained.

Most children are active enough during this period that their appetite improves over what it was during toddlerhood, when their growth tapered off severely, and so did their need for food. This exacerbated Sara's problem with her grandma. At age fifteen months, Sara was responding to a natural decline in appetite. Grandma, though, wanted the little girl to continue eating at the prior pace.

Neither Marsha nor Tom Jasper possessed what one might call a chunky build. Equally significant neither did other males in the extended family. Body build based upon genetics is never a certainty. A friend of mine who stands six-feet-three and weighs, at best, a hundred and eighty pounds, has a mother four-feet-eleven, a father five-feet-eleven, and a brother five-feet-ten. The brother has a weight problem, but neither the friend nor the parents ever did. Generally speaking, though, body type and build *tend* to follow family lines.

Emotional responses may well be passed from parent to child pretty much by observation and osmosis apart from genetics, so obesity *can* run in families when there is no genetic basis. In short, a multitude of factors determine a child's weight versus height, eating patterns, exercise habits, and appearance.

The issue, of course, is not all these other children but yours. You can identify some early indicators that your child might be subject to a lifetime of weight problems. The first question to ask is:

1. Are you obese?

If you suffer from weight problems—if you're consistently underweight or overweight for your height and bone structure (it doesn't matter whether that weight is the result of genes or emotional difficulties)—your child can slide into the same groove you are in.

One of the best things you can do for your child now is to identify the source of your own problem and seek counseling to prevent that source's influence on your child. Whether or not you can resolve your problem, you can head it off in your child.

2. How does your child look?

If your child seems heavier than others of the same age and has a round, pudgy face and plump legs and arms, consult a pediatrician. The child may be taking in more calories than he or she can burn. The number of meals and snacks is not the primary issue here. Small children eat frequently, for they have no storage to speak of. It's the cumulative total through the day that's important.

3. What does your child do?

Jenny Lawton shrugged. "Sara runs and climbs."

Marsha Jasper shrugged. "Brian runs and climbs."

Same answer, but there is a wide disparity between the two children's levels of activity. Sara literally went through her day like that drum-beating, battery-charged bunny in the television commercials. Brian ran and climbed, yes, but not much. He sat a lot, playing with blocks and books. And he discovered television.

To be truthful, he didn't find it on his own. Marsha deliberately hooked him on television. She considered television a wonderful device for keeping the child out of her hair while she prepared meals, did household chores, and met other obligations. Television, she believes, is a wonderful device for educating pre-readers, what with "Sesame Street" and other such programs. To her, television was a wonderful device for keeping Brian out of mischief and keeping him from getting underfoot.

Television is terrible! Certainly it does all those baby-sitting and educational jobs mentioned above, but at a heavy cost. Researchers have been looking lately, not just at the effect television violence, for example, has on children, but also on the actual physical effects of television watching.

You see, small children's eyes do not focus well on details. This is why primary readers have large print. The children's vision is not developed well enough to discern small letters. And yet, the television screen requires adult-level eye control. The screen remains at one fixed distance; small children's eyes (and adults' also, to a lesser extent) are built to look afar and close and in between, flitting from focus to focus. Also, small children are programmed to be moving almost constantly. Right now they need that motion and activity to tune their motor skills. Small children must get plenty of interaction with other people every day in order to develop social and language skills.

Television viewing prevents all that. The physical effects of sitting there watching the small figures on the stationary screen simply are not good for preschoolers. Period. Neither is the inactivity and the lack of social contact. Overweight small children and television watching go hand in hand.

Marsha really ought to give up her electronic babysitter. It will cost her some time, attention, and distraction, but it will be well worth the sacrifice.

Let us assume for the moment that you see tendencies in your child toward being overweight. Possibly, your pediatrician confirms them. There are steps you can take.

Monitoring Weight from the Start

Diet. You already know about minimizing fat content, reducing sugary foods, and promoting raw fruits and vegetables in your child's diet. Try some of the excellent sugar-free fruit spreads now on the market. Flavored yogurt also does well as a bread spread. For drink treats, try mixing club soda with fruit juices.

Marsha objected. "Brian has already come to expect his ice cream after dinner. I end up giving him peanut butter and jelly on bread a lot because he turns down fruit. He hates apples and doesn't like orange slices much. Pears aren't in season very long, and he's not that hot on them anyway. Or bananas. I tried the fruit route, and it didn't work. He insists on his sugary snacks."

Brian's taste buds, frankly, had already been subverted. Sugar will do that. Children are born with a natural skill at balancing foods for good nutrition, providing themselves, if given the choice, with the necessary fats, proteins, and carbohydrates. Sugar becomes, in a sense, addictive. It supplants that natural ability to balance diet.

Marsha stands a far better chance of weaning Brian off too much sugar now, while his diet is completely under her control, than when he gets out into the big, bad world with all its temptations.

"But what do I do when he refuses fruit and insists on jelly or candy?"

Pleasantly inform him it's fruit or nothing, and stick with it. Within a month or two, he will develop healthier habits.

"How do I tell him he can't have ice cream after dinner?"

I recommend pronouncing the words carefully, in English.

Children of this age love to feed themselves. The more you put out a variety of healthy, easy-to-eat snacks and meal portions, the better the diet to which your child will become accustomed . . . and the easier it will be for your child to maintain those good eating habits through life.

Incidentally, don't restrict snacks at this age. You may want to reduce their size, but they are needed to keep the little furnace going. Limiting intake to three meals a day puts too much space between stokings.

Along with a good diet comes exercise—the other key to weight maintenance.

Exercise. "Oh, yeah, right. Exercise. Sara needs more activity like I need more pimples." Jenny blew a raspberry.

No, Sara didn't need any more activity. She was hyperactive as it was. But Brian did. Marsha and Tom would do well to devise some method by which Brian would have maximum opportunity for active play.

A fenced backyard is a wonderful place for small children. The fence keeps the child in, but equally important it protects them by keeping out such potential hazards as stray dogs and unruly older children.

An acquaintance claims, "When our Grace was small we lived in a narrow town house in Philadelphia. No backyard, just a broad cement apron out by the back door. So we put one of those twenty-foot-by-eight-foot dog runs out there—you know, cyclone fence on a pipe frame. It had a wire roof, and it was only four feet high, but that was all right. Gracie was two feet high. Some of the neighbors didn't like it, but I checked building codes and it was legal. She spent hours out there with her blocks and sandbox and tricycle."

Minimizing or eliminating television works wonders in increasing physical activity. Marsha paled at the thought. She protested that Brian had his favorite programs, and she was loathe to force him to give them up.

But at that age, Brian liked the distraction and diversion, not *Gilligan's Island* as such.

Control Issues. This is the biggie, the foundation of emotionally based eating disorders. You can control nearly every facet of a small child's life except that one; you cannot make a small child eat.

Before her third birthday approached, little Sara Lawton was an old hand at driving her grandma nuts. She need only clamp her mouth shut to stymie her grandma. It was the only control issue the child could hope to win, so she played it to the max.

Compounding the picture, Grandma used treats as bribes, in part to elicit desired behaviors and in part to get more calories down Sara's throat. Further compounding the picture, Sara and her mom lived in the grandparents' house. When that occurs, the grandparents *always* take over as parents of all, no matter how old the adult child may be. So long as Jenny stayed under that roof, her parents would rule both Sara and her. Grandma's will would prevail over Mommy's.

Sara was impossible to keep at the table during Jenny and her parents' evening meals. Jenny felt powerful unspoken pressure from her parents, especially her mother, to make Sara behave and eat. That is, Sara was expected to conform to Grandma's idea of what constituted good behavior. Unfortunately, Grandma refused to acknowledge that Sara was one of those children who simply cannot sit still.

And what did Sara do? The opposite, of course!

Count on it.

How do you reverse a control issue? Any change must be initiated with the adult. The child has absolutely no ability to alter an escalating situation. Children are reactors, not actors.

Jenny would have no luck changing Sara's course until and unless either her mother cooperated in the changes or Jenny and Sara moved out. Now, control issues have a way of gripping adults in a death lock too. Jenny's mom simply could not let go. She *had* to have her way, *had* to make Sara eat more, *had* to show who was the stronger. Reasoning and protests reached her at head level, but she would quickly revert to her old habits because the heart was still in there trying to control Sara.

Jenny's father was not hung up on that particular control problem. When he finally got fed up with the fighting and tears at every single meal, he drew the line.

"No more of this!"

Jenny's mom was hurt and furious. But Jenny seized the opportunity to adopt practices her parenting group had suggested and, until now, she'd been unable to try.

1. She eliminated food bribes.

She substituted opportunities to go out and run and climb some more, an extra trip to the playground, a stroll to the park.

2. She let Sara leave the table when she wanted to.

This really bothered Grandma, but Grandpa basked in the new peace and quiet.

3. She avoided letting food become a control issue by allowing Sara to eat on demand.

Jenny kept the uneaten portion of Sara's dinners in the refrigerator. When Sara got hungry later, Jenny pulled out the dinner plate and invited Sara to dig in. Sara didn't seem to notice that it was cold, and the cold food in her tummy, particularly at this older age, didn't cause any problems.

In making food a non-issue, Jenny fed Sara when the child was hungry. Sometimes that meant that Sara ate before the rest of the household. Jenny was wise to lean a little in the opposite direction, causing temporary disruption in meal schedules in order to tip Sara away from the control aspects of eating. Things would even out later.

Physical growth depends greatly upon food and exercise, yes, but sleep is also an important factor. Sleep habits vary widely with age. Newborns sleep most of the time. Little children need naps. And sleep habits, too, can easily become another pesky control issue.

Sleep Patterns

"Control issue? You better believe it." Jenny grimaced. "Sara hates going to bed at night. Hates it! Besides, you'd think something with sides as high as Sara's crib would keep a kid locked up safely. Not Sara. We lowered the bed as far as it would go and she *still* crawled up and out. Landed on her head a couple of times. She was determined to get out of there, and Mom was determined to keep her in."

Jenny's dad suggested a drop lid for the crib, like a car hood. Cage the kid in. Jenny's mom said something about a youth bed, and how Jenny had one at two and a half.

Sometime during late toddler age, most children graduate from their crib to a bed. For some, this move can lead to problems because the child, suddenly living a dream fulfilled, can get up at will.

Parents meet that problem in various ways—from a

stern blanket order: "Once you're in bed, you stay there unless the smoke alarm goes off" to a lock on the inside of the parents' bedroom door. (Nothing quells passion quicker than an unexpected little voice opening the door and cooing, "Mommy?")

Youth beds are all right if you wish, but shifting from a crib to a regular twin-size bed is just as effective and less costly. It may not be possible to allow the child to have a room alone; few small children have that option. If the child is given the corner of an older sibling's room, or even if your two-year-old *is* the older sibling, the child may actually sleep better. Being alone at this age can be scary. If children do share a room, the portion of the room in which each child's bed sits is that child's and that child's alone. Children, even small ones, are very territorial.

I strongly recommend against any child but a newborn sleeping in the parents' bedroom. If yours is a one-bedroom apartment, sacrifice gracious *House Beautiful* living and set up the crib in the living room or dining room.

Because the child's general health and well-being depend so heavily upon good and sufficient rest, let me offer some suggestions for getting past control fights and making bedtime a pleasant experience.

Switching from Crib to Bed

Ah, what a ceremony this invites, rather like launching the *Queen Mary*. You might wish to mark the occasion with a sheet cake decorated with a dollhouse crib and bed; juice, maybe, drunk from the disposable stemware you find at wedding supply stores; a special meal or an unveiling ceremony.

Furnish the child's new bed with linens and covers appropriate for a preschooler—a dinosaur comforter, perhaps, Noah's ark, or bright farm animals. Gestures of this sort tell the child, *This is grown-up stuff, and it is yours alone. You are special!* Powerful message!

Sara, with her Houdini act, was more than ready to exchange crib for bed. Brian Jasper, though, could remain longer in his crib, in part because he was expressing his growing up in other ways and in part because he was not terribly discontent there.

This is not to suggest that Brian enjoyed going to bed at night. Hardly. When Tom and Marsha were staring glassy-eyed at life, Brian was still going strong. Nine, nine-thirty, ten at night. What is an appropriate bedtime for a preschooler?

Seven. Seven-thirty.

The child needs the sleep. Yes. But even more, the parents need time together without the distraction of the child. We are concerned with the child's emotional and psychological health, but that also depends upon the parents' emotional renewal.

Tom would protest, "But a lot of days, I don't get home until nearly seven. I wouldn't have any time with him."

It's an excellent point. May I suggest that Marsha should have Brian fed, night-diapered if diapers are still in the picture, and prepared for bed in every way. The bed itself is prepared, the covers turned down and waiting. Marsha reads Brian a story and plays with him. When Tom arrives, he takes over as Marsha prepares supper. Tom also reads Brian a story and plays with him. You certainly won't find Brian objecting to the duplication. Tom tucks him in, then his evening with his wife and lover begins.

When Tom protested, "I wouldn't have any time with

him," it was equally true that he wouldn't have any quiet, effective, satisfying, nurturing time with Marsha either. There must be balance and intimate contact—and I don't mean hasty lovemaking at midnight.

If Tom is *really* late, Marsha might tuck Brian into bed, say at seven-thirty, with the admonition, "Now don't go to sleep yet. Daddy will be home soon and he wants to read to you."

If Brian has had a rough day, the reverse psychology may work well and he'll go right off. Perhaps—nay, probably—he will indeed still be wide-eyed when Daddy gets in. In either case, going to bed without Daddy is neither onerous nor a punishment. It is a normal event. (Conservative little creatures, children thrive on routine.) There is no pressure to sleep.

That Control Issue

Marsha cannot make Brian go to sleep anyway. No one can. Sleep can become a control issue in the same way food can and for the same reason: The child is in control.

Tom and Marsha can control the bedtime. What Brian does is up to him.

In the illustration above, Marsha avoided allowing bedtime to become a control problem by letting Brian choose his own sleep pattern. She set the stage according to a routine and then let go.

In the Lawtons' home, Grandma could not let go. When Grandma tried to make Sara go to sleep, Sara responded by escaping the moment she could. Grandma refused to let Sara have any toys in her crib, fearing that the distraction of play would somehow keep little Sara awake. Cribs are for sleeping in, not playing in, Grandma insisted. We certainly wouldn't want little Sara thinking she could play instead of getting down to the serious business of sleeping.

Obviously, Sara did not share those sentiments.

Grandma needn't worry about it. In fact, a few tactile toys might promote sleep. A favorite doll, a furry stuffed animal, one of those soft rubber balls that looks like a startled sea urchin (Koosh® balls, do they call them?) . . . because the preschooler is so much more alert to tactile sensation than we are, those kinds of textured toys will invite stroking, repetitive rubbing, clinging, and hugging. All such actions promote drowsiness.

I'm sure I needn't bother to mention that you must never make going to bed a form of punishment. That would be counterproductive to the extreme.

The Goal of Bedtime

Remember the goals we set up for parenting? They apply here. Bedtime is a teaching situation. You want to teach your child to function independently, and that includes being able to soothe himself or herself in order to go to sleep. Plush animals, dolls, and other toys are means to an end. With them the child can practice and perfect the skill of self-pacifying.

Keep that goal in mind.

The Joy of Routine

As much as Brian Jasper would fight to be allowed to stay up, down inside, he relished the routine of a standard bedtime. More than anything else, a routine encourages regular sleep habits.

Allowing Brian to stay up until nine-thirty or ten, the habit the Jaspers had fallen into, was not really routine. It was resistance to routine on everyone's part. What sort of routine, if any, could make Brian the least bit amenable to a bedtime two hours earlier?

1. Sleep clothes that differ from play clothes

Sleepers, pajamas, a different T-shirt—whatever Brian wears to bed, it should be reserved for bedtime only. Here's a strong nonverbal signal that playtime has ended. We're shifting modes.

2. A preparation routine

Preparation includes brushing teeth, washing the face, or taking a warm, soothing bath. What you and your child do to prepare for bed will be governed as much by family traditions as need. I remember in the old, old film *The Yearling,* with Gregory Peck in the father's role, the son, Claude Jarman, wore a shirt and pants with suspenders. When he went to bed, the boy took off his pants, his feet already bare, and crawled into bed in his shirt.

In my own youth I yearned for the utter simplicity of that. That film character had pared bedtime to the raw essentials. A two-year-old benefits from a bit more trimming to the basic act.

3. Bedtime treats

Bedtime treats need not be food. They might include a game, unstructured play time, or feeding the goldfish. Bedtime play should not be too exciting and rambunctious. A cup of warm milk does much to promote drowsiness.

4. A wind-down routine

Every week at the close of a friend's daughter's ballet class, the instructor leads a brief eight-step routine ending in a sweeping and gracious bow. All the students master the routine. The class does not end willy-nilly, you see. It ends with that deep bow. Closure . . . an act that declares, *That was instruction. Now instruction is ended.* Similarly, a local square dance band, regardless of the kinds of dances they have been playing all evening, always ends with a slow fox-trot, "Good Night, Ladies." Always. There is no question that the evening is over.

This is the sort of closure to the day the Jaspers ought to use. By age two, Brian had a few books he adored and listened to over and over. At least one of them ought to be reserved as the last story before bed. Children don't mind hearing the same thing a million times. A special story told as the final thing before sleep says, "It's time to end the day."

A friend named Sandi, as her act of closure, put her child down, said good night, kissed the child's forehead, kissed a stuffed bear's forehead, held the bear's nose to the child's cheek and made a kissing sound, and tucked the bear in with the child. Invariably. On those occasions when they were on the road, at the grandparents' or in a motel, the routine remained the same. The bear got pretty threadbare.

"We lived in northern Maine," says Sandi. "That means that in the summer, the girls were going to bed in broad daylight. We used the heavy black window shades day-sleepers use. In winter it got dark at four, and the kids were asleep on their feet from five o'clock on. We had to work to keep them up 'til seven-thirty. Light makes a big difference."

It does indeed. Make sure your child goes to sleep in a room with reduced light. Window shades or heavy curtains can block summer sun. Small children will appreciate a soft night-light, however.

5. Don't abandon; reassure

Think about the unspoken messages you deliver when you tell your child you will check on him or her now and then. Of course, then you must not neglect to do so. This checking in will not be a stern, "Now go to sleep!" or an accusatory, "Aren't you asleep yet?" It will simply be a smile and a touch, perhaps a soothing word or kiss. The child, remember, instinctively appreciates a touch. Checking in is also a good safety precaution and should be done whenever Mom or Dad wakes up in the night.

Notice I did not advocate picking up the child. The object is to help the child relax for sleep. Picking up excites. Even more, when a parent picks up a child, it is the parent soothing the child; the child is not learning how to soothe himself or herself.

Should the Jaspers faithfully follow a routine with those elements, bedtime will likely smooth out considerably at the earlier hour within three or four weeks. A fully established routine, engaged in with élan by the parents, works beautifully.

Sheer lack of sleep is one of the biggest problems very small children can have. People who know claim that, statistically, adults don't get nearly enough good rest at night to function well through the day, and neither do children. Sound health and bright spirits depend upon good rest.

Children do not always sleep angelically through the night, of course. Disruptions occur.

Waking in the Night

"She was sitting bolt upright in bed, wide awake, and screaming!" Jenny described her terrifying first encounter with Sara's nightmares. "I mean screaming. She was absolutely certain it was real, but she never could explain what it was."

Nightmares

That's common in nightmares. A few such dreams persist in memory. Most do not. They intrude, they terrify, and then they fly. Nightmares are one of the ways a child's brain processes unsettling or unusual information. That information might be scary stories, movies, or television programs. It might be something unnerving to the child that we adults consider so routine we think nothing of it.

"I held her and rocked her back and forth," Jenny continued, "and talked to her. But it was maybe ten minutes before she settled down enough to go back to bed. I was going to take her into bed with me, but then I thought, no, I better not."

Good instincts. Jenny handled it just right. Reassure. Hold tightly. Hug. Rock. Soothe. You can explain it was a bad dream, but don't devalue the child's terror with something like, "Oh, that wasn't really scary," or "Nothing to worry about." It certainly *was* scary!

Night Terrors

Brian Jasper experienced a different phenomenon. When he sat bolt upright screaming, Marsha rushed to pick him up. But he didn't wake up. In fact, Marsha could not wake him up. Eventually, he settled back to fitful rest, still unawakened. In the morning, he had no recollection or interest in what happened during the night.

Night terrors, we believe (but we aren't sure), are some sort of short circuit, so to speak, in the brain. It may be neurochemical. At any rate, the child does not remember anything about it afterward. The child experiencing a nightmare will awaken and remember, if not the dream itself, at least that it occurred. Not so with night terrors.

Night terrors usually end spontaneously by about first grade.

Normally night awakenings are infrequent. If your child develops a pattern of awakening frequently, perhaps even several nights in a row, you might want to contact your pediatrician. Your child might be responding to some stressful situation that needs further examination.

Sleepwalking

It comes as something of a shock, the first time your pajama-clad child walks out into the living room like a zombie. A sleepwalker looks like, well, a sleepwalker. The child may or may not wake up. Children who awaken in strange surroundings tend to take the incongruity a little better than do adults; after all, small children fall asleep anywhere and wake up anywhere. How often has your child fallen asleep in the carseat after leaving the mall, only to wake up in your driveway or living room or in his or her own bed?

Gently lead the child back to bed. Reassure, and don't ridicule, then or later.

Miscellaneous Reasons

Young children, just like adults, wake up in the middle of the night for a whole host of miscellaneous reasons.

"I'm hungry." "I'm thirsty." "I have to go to the bathroom." "I don't feel good." "I just remembered something."

If such reasons are valid for you when you wake up, they're equally valid for your child. Especially pay attention if your child complains of not feeling well. Illnesses inconveniently and all too frequently begin during the night.

You could be the culprit awakening the child during the night. As potty training commences, you may want to actually get your child up for a potty try before you go to bed.

Potty training . . . ultimately, child and adult both survive the process, but during its throes, child and adult together may wonder whether they will.

Toilet Training

Once upon a time, when mothers vied arduously for the crown of perfection, toilet training was the master measure. Women boasted of success at eighteen months.

"Ah, but my little Sylvester trained at a year—as soon as he could walk."

"That's very nice, but my darling Mehitabel would tell me when she was six months old and I'd sit her on the potty, and voilá!"

Left in the dust were the poor mothers of dolts who failed to potty train well until they were two and a half to three years old. Actually, those poor mothers weren't nearly as bad off as they thought. They were the only ones who really did possess potty-trained children.

You see, a child's sphincter control and tone are usually not adequate to hold it until at least the age of two. Both the anal and urinal sphincters are controlled by tiny muscles served by tiny nerves. Babies cannot feel when it's happening, and even toddlers who get the idea cannot physically maintain control. Statistically, girls have a bit of an edge over boys; most girls develop enough control to train well by about two and a half years of age. Boys may go as long as three years or later, and that is perfectly normal. Don't despair.

The miasma of diapers being what it is, parents are understandably anxious to see early and complete success. This leads to a temptation to push the child, cajoling for performance or even punishing for infraction. The truth is, most children readily engage in the adventure of becoming big people and will train as soon as they can handle it. Those children who resist training are *not* going to respond well to pushing. Forcing the matter before the child is physically capable of succeeding will only delay success.

Little children do not want to remain in diapers when none of the adults and older children they know—or house pets, incidentally—wear them. When parents lead the way to graduation out of diapers, providing the necessary potty and panties, the children eagerly participate. They are not as hungry for success as are the parents, but they are certainly ready to make the change. Wise parents provide the accoutrements and instruction and sit back, relaxing, letting nature take its course.

The first welcome sign, not unlike a few swallows showing up at Capistrano, is when the child is able to associate urination or defecation with a physical feeling. The parent catches on that this has happened by observing in the child a facial expression or sudden cessation of activity. Some children may actually tell their parents when they are soiling a diaper.

"Ah-hah!" cries the diaper-weary parent. "It's time!"

Perhaps not. At this point, although now ready to

meet a toilet, the child may not be physically ready yet—that is, have the physical control—actually to be trained.

Now, however, is the time to buy a potty chair. It will help matters along if your child can become familiar with it in advance of need and understand its function.

Headstrong little Sara's beleaguered grandmother did not believe in associating potty chairs with play. Potty time was serious business, just as bedtime was. This was not a time for fun or distraction. Grandmas, especially old-fashioned grandmas, tend to take the serious things of life quite seriously while small children take nothing and everything seriously. Predictably, toilet training became still another control issue between Sara and her caregiver. Grandma controlled the potty chair. But she failed to remember who controlled the bowel movements.

Remember that a small child does not reason things out. Most (some say all) of what we think about is thought about verbally rather than with mental pictures. A small child cannot think abstractly because his or her language is not yet advanced enough and mental pictures are too hard to conjure; after all, the child has no background of memories yet to draw from.

So children play out their questions and answers about life with physical action. No moment of a small child's play is idle pursuit the way moments of play—games, mindless TV watching, light reading—are with adults. Play is the child's work, the child's exploration of life, the child's growth.

When the child makes dolly "pee-pee" in the potty, the child is playing out serious questions about the purpose of the potty chair. When the child sits on the chair, that is literally rehearsal for the main event . . . not thinking it out mentally but thinking it out physically.

Sooner or later, that main event will begin, both thrilling and frustrating everyone involved. Some guidelines will make the process as smooth as possible.

1. Keep the potty accessible at all times.

A small child, heaven knows, has no capacity to wait. "Now" means *now!* For the first few months, take the potty chair along on trips and outings, to the neighbors'— wherever possible. The secret word here is *handy*.

"We did that. You know how now and then some surreal scene comes along that sticks with you forever?" Our friend Sandi was overstating it a bit with her *forever*, but I understood her point. "While our daughter was potty training, we happened to be traveling across West Texas in a VW square back. It was the middle of May, so it was pretty warm. The windows were down. And there is our daughter in the back of the square back like the Queen of the Nile, sitting on her potty chair and smelling dust and looking at a herd of pronghorn antelope fifty feet from the road. She doesn't remember it, she says, but I sure do."

2. Put your child in training pants as soon as you start training.

The child must learn to drop the drawers quickly when the need arises. That takes plenty of practice. Also, a child cannot undo diapers. Besides, the training pants signal the Big Change. Night diapers will be necessary for a while yet; once the child goes to sleep, all control goes out the window. During waking hours, though, put up with the half dozen pairs of wet underpants each day that it will take to get the show on the road.

During the first chaotic days of training, it might be

possible to allow the child to go bare-bottom. The child can simply sit down on the potty when the need arises with no fumbling, and the feel of airy freedom is different enough that the situation bears no resemblance to soiling a diaper.

3. Use diapers when embarrassment will be a factor.

Whose embarrassment? Both yours and your child's. You will be embarrassed if your child cuts loose in the grocery store. The child will be embarrassed if an accident happens, for instance, in front of valued friends and relatives. An alternative for situations of that sort might be disposable training pants, which are particularly absorbent but manageable by tiny beginners.

4. Praise your child's success without making too big a deal of it.

And, of course, never punish for failures. Rarely will the child fail deliberately. Little kids fail a lot. Because there is no good capacity yet to retain wastes, urine especially, the child who is absorbed in some great play adventure will totally forget about things until it's too late. It's not deliberate. It's a baby brain in action. Similarly, the child will not think about it when napping or drowsy. It's all part of the game.

5. Forcing a child to sit on the potty until the desired result occurs works at cross purposes.

Children who have a hard time controlling release have an even harder time performing on cue. Let the skill develop naturally. Besides, you're getting into control issues here, with the undercurrent of, "Whose will will prevail?" That's always a good thing to avoid.

6. As much as possible, keep your distaste out of the picture.

A friend I'll call Bill grinned impishly. "In college, a couple of us biology majors would sit in the cafeteria at mealtime and talk about dissections. Pretty soon the girls sitting nearby would lose their appetite and say, 'Here. You want my dessert?' Or salad, or whatever. We ate like kings. Shucks, that kind of stuff didn't bother us. We were used to it."

Doctors, biologists, emergency-services professionals, slaughterhouse workers, farmers, and a few others are used to it. Excrement and the grosser aspects of life don't faze them. Such enlightened folk, however, are a small minority. For the majority of people, bodily functions and similar topics are a royal turn-off. If it weren't for the mess of diapers, some parents would probably avoid potty training altogether because of its unappetizing, unseemly character.

It will help potty training if you can keep revulsion and distaste under wraps. The child may lose interest in something that is looked upon with disdain or worse by Mommy and Daddy. The child experiences no such distaste. On the contrary, the child will probably exhibit an enthusiastic curiosity. Divert attention, distract, redirect as you wish, but try not to cast as "ugly" the functions with which the child will be concerned for a whole life long.

Approached with the right combination of nonchalance and enthusiasm, potty training should proceed fairly well. When you toilet train your child, you are teaching control over his or her body. That's a big, big step toward independence, one most children embrace eagerly. I could just as easily have put this discussion in the section on separation and individuation.

So what can go wrong? Several things. Should the parents push a child to succeed before control is physically possible, the frustrated child may rebel completely. At the very least, the child will feel an intense sense of failure (and with it a drastic loss of what little self-esteem there is at this age) that is not the child's failure at all. And then there's always that control issue.

When Potty Training Goes Awry

Not only is it unusual for children to wet or soil their pants beyond the age of three and a half or four, there are medical terms for the situation when it occurs. Defecating in pants when potty training should have been complete is called *encopresis*. *Enuresis* is the term for pants-wetting or bed-wetting.

Medical Reasons

Medical reasons should always be the first thought of a parent whose child suffers repeated accidents. Should a medical workup fail to find a physical reason for the problem, then consider a psychological or emotional source.

Control Issues

And then there was Sara. Sara's grandma may have heard that children will train when they're ready, but she was determined to hurry Sara into readiness. Quite likely, at the back of her mind lingered that old traditional mental boast of mothers of yesteryear, "I am a superior parent because my child trained early."

Sara resisted. Grandma persisted.

She tried bribery, setting aside certain toys. "These are big-girl toys for big girls in pants. When you're ready to wear big-girl pants, you can play with these toys."

Actually, bribery like that frequently works if the child is otherwise good and ripe for training. Was Sara? Nope.

Grandma hedged her bet by setting Sara on the potty after meals and naps. When Sara, usually wailing, was eventually allowed up from these attempts, her little bottom would have a big red ring on it. At two and a half, Sara finally had pretty good muscle control. She used it to resist urinating. She could hold it for up to half an hour, releasing only after she was off the pot and back into her training panties.

Was that deliberate? You'd better believe it.

Sara's mother, Jenny, resolved the control struggle between her daughter and her mother by moving out.

Shauna, also a single mother, found a three-bedroom apartment for a reasonable price and invited Jenny and Sara to move in with her and her daughter, Afton. Exhausted by the constant friction between her mother and herself over how Sara should be raised, Jenny accepted. Jenny and Shauna agreed to share childcare expenses, groceries, and rent across the board. It was too good a deal to pass up.

One small fly buzzed around the ointment: Afton was potty trained; Sara was not. So Sara's tuition at the day care home where both girls would stay while their mothers worked cost considerably more than Afton's. Despite the fact that Jenny's mom had been struggling in vain for six months to train Sara, Jenny said brashly, "She'll be out of diapers in two weeks."

She dismissed the bribes, the cajoling, the long sessions sitting on the potty. Instead she casually pointed out that all the other kids in Sara's new day care home, except for the little baby who couldn't walk yet, used the potty. Afton used the potty. Mommy used the potty. Wouldn't it be great when Sara was big enough to use the potty!

No pressure. No chiding about wet panties. No angry or hostile reaction to Sara's habits of elimination. Above all, no desire to impose Jenny's will upon Sara, forcing Sara to bend.

Jenny's estimate of Sara's success was seven days off; she was out of diapers in a week.

4. THE WONDERFUL NEW ME

SEPARATION AND INDIVIDUATION

And you, fathers, do not provoke your children
to wrath, but bring them up in the training
and admonition of the Lord.

THE APOSTLE PAUL (Eph. 6:4)

Brian was two. I'll never forget how all of a sudden he turned into a person instead of a baby. I don't know how to explain it any other way." Marsha Jasper wagged her head. "Maybe it wasn't a transformation; maybe it was there all along and I didn't notice it 'til then."

"I'd call it a transformation," Tom interjected. "When he turned two, I was finally able to relate to him. Before that he seemed like a small creature that only my wife ought to be taking care of. Sure, I'm an enlightened father and all that; doing my share of childcare. But it still seemed like Marsha was the mother and I was the baby-sitter—until now."

"At three," a friend told me, "our Cynthia's personality really started to come through. Where she got it, I don't know. She's certainly her own little person now."

"That kid's got an attitude," said Shauna, describing a neighbor's child. "I don't know what it is, but if he grows up that way, he's either going to end up in a boxing ring or on death row."

While the one- to two-year-old is just beginning to try the waters of independence, wading ankle-deep, the two-to three-year-old has plunged in all the way and the four-year-old is not a little child but a Child. Possessed of a clear personal identity, the two-year-old no longer has to buck the world in order to, by opposing others, establish himself or herself as an individual. That awareness of individuality is comfortably in place. The child is now free to expand and cement this uniqueness.

A well-developed kid from age two and a half on is generally pleasant to be around. Some of the friction and contrariness generated by the innate need to break away, to separate from Mommy and Daddy, will have lessened. Socially more sophisticated, the child can get along fairly well with most other human beings around him or her, not just with Mommy or Daddy.

During these next few years of life, the child solidifies a relationship with others, to an extent, but he or she solidifies far more a relationship with *self.* The tasks of the former years were to build relationships with the primary caretaker and the immediate family and then to emerge from that unit; by this time, those relationships are complete. Now the healthy child can shift the focus to himself or herself.

In solid relationship with Mommy and Daddy, little Brian Jasper blossomed. At his primal preschool level, he mixed sweetness and aggressiveness into a self who could get whatever he wanted with charm and diplomacy. Well, almost whatever.

Sara Lawton, too, felt comfortable with herself. She had developed a solid bond with Mommy and a vigorous adversarial bond with her primary caregiver, her grandmother. Both bonds performed their necessary job of helping Sara differentiate herself as a unique individual with her own wants. A bond is a bond. Even as they locked in battles of wits and control, Sara and Grandma knew each other intimately and demonstrated amply that they were separate people.

Sara lacked a father figure. I detest that term, "father figure," as if Daddy were a statue out in the garden to be displayed and admired. An involved daddy is an important key to the child's growth. The fact was, Sara lacked a daddy. She had Grandpa, but Grandpa, uneasy about his relationship with the tiny girl and deeply disappointed by Jenny's unwed motherhood, kept a certain emotional distance that was not in Sara's best interests.

Sara could make it without a daddy (or without a mommy; if an unwed father were her primary caregiver, the principles would remain the same). It will be more difficult, however, and Sara's development may lag until she is a little older and able to seek further afield for people who can help shape her—beyond the immediate family to day care workers and peers, extended family and friends.

But development must not lag too much or that window of opportunity will slip by. The opportunity pertinent to this age is:

HELP YOUR CHILD ESTABLISH A STRONG, HEALTHY SELF-IDENTITY.

This is not a thing parents and other primary caretakers can consciously teach children. Like the imbuing of trust, it comes or doesn't come according to the child's experiences with life. But it comes through specific avenues. The child has divided away from the parents to become an individual, a separate lump from the family clay. Now is the time to instill in that individual a sense of value and respect, shaping the clay into beauty.

To illustrate building value and respect at this preschool level, I would like to use the young man I alluded to briefly in Chapter 1. This is Winona's son, Ben, age twelve, who, Winona suspected, was smoking behind her back. I'm using a twelve-year-old in part so you can see the effects of not building the child's self-identity in the preschool years.

Building Respect and Value

Ben Schatz knew when he wasn't wanted. Following dinner, his father, Edward, had said simply, "Go do your homework." Mom and Dad remained at the table sipping coffee. Obviously, they were going to talk, and equally obviously, they would be talking about him. Later, he knew from experience, they would talk *at* him.

He grabbed his backpack where he'd dropped it out in the foyer and trundled off to his room. But he didn't do his homework. He fiddled around with his Game Boy awhile. He thumbed through a book on chess strategies, but he knew that until he set up the board, he wouldn't get much out of it. He had to look at the field and actually move the pieces while he read in order to grab the gist of the text. He was doing really well on the school chess team, with a 5-0-0 record in intramural play, but his dad still wouldn't let him set up the chess board at home. "You don't waste time playing games until your grades come up, hear me? Apply yourself to things that are worth something," Dad said.

Ben's math teacher, Mr. Gates, doubled as chess coach. He didn't think chess was a waste of time at all. Ben liked Mr. Gates's assessment of the game better than his dad's. Mr. Gates would get Ben passes and fix it up so he could work out chess problems during study halls since he couldn't do it at home.

From out in the living room, Dad yelled Ben's name. Ben sighed. *Here it came.* They'd talked it over—a united front, Mom called it—and now they were going to explain to Ben how he was falling short. Again. With an expletive and another sigh, he tossed the chess book back in his bag and strolled out to the living room.

Not only were Ben's parents failing to grant him the status commensurate with his emerging adolescence—that's near-adulthood, you realize—they weren't even treating him the way you'd handle a preschooler. Their tactics did nothing to encourage him now, and those same unchanged tactics hadn't worked back when he was two-and-some, either. So let's pretend that not only would Edward and Winona reverse their methods, but also that they had done so back when Ben was three or four. Would that have relieved their problems now, and if so, how much?

Give the Child Full Family Status

As you deal with discipline questions and behavior limits throughout your child's life, you'll want to do as Edward and Winona did in one important respect: present a united front. They never argued in front of the children about a course of action. For example, should bedtime be enforced rigidly or casually? They discussed that when Ben was two, came to agreement, and as far as Ben knew, that's the way it was. He had no idea that his parents at first disagreed strongly, then reached a compromise.

But most of parenting is not argument and compromise. It's working out details of a complex tangle of relationships. Many families establish a regular pattern of family meetings in which children and adults together discuss needs, schedules, and situations.

Certainly an adult takes charge of meetings of this sort, at least in the beginning, but the children receive a respectful hearing. Their opinions are considered and their wishes are granted when possible. Most of all, a family meeting must be a forum, not just one more opportunity for the parents to rag on the kids. In fact, correction and discipline should be banned from the table. Later, as children enter the upper grades, the family meeting will provide an excellent venue for meshing the highly complex activities schedules that children that age always manage to generate.

As a two-year-old Ben should have been invited to participate in the family, whether or not family meetings were held. And absolutely, Ben, as a twelve-year-old, should have been included in decision-making sessions. Summarily dismissing him, as his father routinely did, sent the powerful message that his opinion—his very presence— was not worth considering. He was a troublesome addendum to the family, not a part of it. That does nothing to foster self-respect and a sense of value.

Include your preschooler in the family as much as possible? In actual decision-making? Certainly, for the child's sake.

Care, and Then Express That Care

I shouldn't have to even mention such a thing. But look at the relationship between Ben and his parents. Affection was there, and his parents genuinely cared, but very little of those feelings were openly expressed. Frankly, Winona was even worse about this than Edward. Ben had to earn affection; he had to deserve displays of affection, and in his parents' eyes, those deserving times were few and far between.

As insecure as a twelve-year-old can be, a preschooler is more so. A preschooler requires nearly constant expressions of affection. These need not all be roaring hugs and juicy kisses. A pat, a rub of the head, a happy word will do between the tumultuous hugs and kisses. The twelve-year-old may be deeply embarrassed by expressions of affection, but that doesn't mean he or she doesn't understand and value them. The preschooler is not embarrassed; the preschooler thrives on them.

Caring implies a relationship, and that is where the Schatzes fell down. Nothing else matters as much as relationship.

Never Stop Building a Relationship

The preschool Ben and the twelve-year-old Ben share an important need, the need to be recognized as a person outside the immediate family. It is not as strong in the preschooler's case, but it's there. In the twelve-year-old's case, Ben must bridge the chasm between belonging to the family and going out into the world away from the family. He would do that by building a strong relationship with a person outside the family while Ben himself was still under his family's aegis. He did that with Mr. Gates.

Ben was among a number of children in his middle school who took up chess seriously. To them it was more than just a game, the way basketball or football is more than just a game in some regions. Had Ben's interest gone to football his father would have supported it. Fathers support sons who play football. But Ben's father failed to see chess as a pastime that was just as demanding as contact sports. Most importantly, Edward did not know and understand Ben well enough to see the boy's interest and aptitude.

The relationship that would have seen Ben and his dad through this rough time should have started from the beginning, two years before even the two-year-old needed it. Remember Anna, zooming around the countryside in her kiddy carseat beside her daddy? Remember Brian Jasper, curled up on his daddy's lap, reading a story? And Sara, in the grocery cart at age three, talking a mile a minute to Jenny as they shopped?

But preschoolers need another avenue of growth involving relationship, an avenue the infant and toddler do not need. Children of preschool age need contact with peers and adults outside the family. This is a new wrinkle with important socialization overtones. But it is also a relationship builder. What kind of contact is this? A brief nursery-school situation. A parents' night out. Supervised play with friends.

Find and Praise the Child's Strengths

It is so easy to build a strong sense of achievement in preschoolers. They are mastering so many skills during this age that achievements come tumbling one after the other.

Brian Jasper was a particularly easy kid to praise. He worked doggedly to get the hang of dressing himself. He didn't quite master it, but he needed remarkably little help. Marsha got him Velcro-closure shoes so he wouldn't have to butt heads with shoelaces. Shirts and overalls inside out? Nothing worth mentioning. Brian looked a bit odd some days? No problem. A seamstress who made most of her own clothes, Marsha made Brian shirts with big, easy snaps in front. In short, she encouraged the things he could do, making them easier, just so he could enjoy plenty of victories over life.

Tom and Marsha recognized in their son a fierce desire to master skills, to achieve perfection. To temper that tendency they lavished praise on imperfection and partial mastery so long as it was his best effort.

Sara gave up on projects if she did not succeed with them quickly. Jenny would have to praise her efforts as well as her achievements, cheering her on and encouraging her to stick with it. Not browbeating, certainly. Cheering. Helping without interfering was a skill Jenny had a real problem mastering. She wanted to just grab it and do it. Sara gave up too easily to allow Jenny that option.

"Ben? What did he ever do at age two that would merit praise?" Edward Schatz might say. Edward always jacked up his expectations a bit higher than Ben's capabilities. By doing so, Edward thought he was encouraging his son to have higher standards. Actually he was doing quite the opposite. By the close of age two, Ben had given up thinking he could do anything.

Edward noticed every shortcoming he could think of. You see, Edward and Winona both were certain that Ben could be perfect if only his shortcomings were pointed out so he could quickly eliminate them.

"Oh, that's nonsense!" Winona might say if her attitude were expressed to her in just those words. "Nobody's perfect."

In the light of day, they do sound like nonsense. They *are* nonsense. But down deep, that's the attitude Ben's parents harbored. And the attitude began not as Ben entered junior high but when he entered his third year.

At age three (in fact, at two) he mastered the tricycle and climbing stairs one foot per step. He ate well with knife and fork, cleaned up toys and messes without too much badgering, and let Aunt Kate kiss him (a big step forward—Aunt Kate scared the willies out of him). His parents recognized none of those victories.

In truth, Ben achieved mightily at age twelve also. He kept his grades up in the C range despite a total lack of effective support at home. (His sister made A's. That made A's not just the goal but the norm. Anything less was substandard.) He stayed clean and sober in a school where drugs and alcohol circulated freely. And he played inspired chess. Beautiful chess. He was a good kid. But his parents didn't notice that, so Ben didn't notice. In his own eyes, he was nothing. To teachers and friends' parents he was a model child, and the Schatzes were sure lucky to have him.

Treat Mistakes with Grace

Never in his life, at two or at twelve, did Ben even once fail to hear about any mistakes he made. Sara's grandma shared the same blind spot Ben's parents did. She saw every error. Furthermore, when Grandma spilled something it was an accident; when Sara spilled something she was either clumsy, careless, naughty, or all of the above.

Preschoolers make an incredible number of mistakes. Their lack of coordination and their unawareness of where their body parts are and what they're doing work against them, of course. So does their lack of experience with the laws of physics—what happens when you throw, bump, stack, lurch, reach. This is a time when they need to learn by trial and error.

We adults are told that we should consider errors to be learning experiences. Yeah, sure. But small children really do learn this way. If only the adult will take a child's errors and accidents in the same light, dismissing mistakes for the learning attempts that they are, the child will benefit greatly. Self-respect will not suffer a bit, the child's relationship with the adult will profit, and the child will have learned whatever that error teaches.

Consider the attitude of a progressive school I heard about. A visitor to the school noticed the students doing math with ink pens.

"Isn't that unusual to use a pen for your math problems?" he asked one of the kids.

"No," was the reply.

Another child pulled out a paper with a bunch of red circles around some of her answers. "Look at all the things I need to learn," the child said with a bright, excited look.

Wrong answers? Not for long.

Let Kids Express Feelings

Ben's household was typical of so many I've dealt with in counseling. When Ben's dad blew up, he had every reason to. However, Ben's mom wasn't supposed to get angry with Dad, and she expressed anger toward Ben only when Dad was absent. Ben and his sister never, ever had any valid reason to voice anger. In short, nobody rocked Dad's boat except Dad himself.

Certainly Ben would never dream of expressing overt anger toward his dad. Unthinkable. And yet he seethed beneath the surface. Part of the lack of relationship in that family was the powerful undercurrent of unspoken feelings, both good and bad.

Back when Ben was two, he should have been learning through his parents' example and guidance to recognize, voice, and resolve feelings of all sorts. Those same examples and guidance would help Ben find a safe middle ground between repressing intense feelings and blowing wild. If the parents had allowed free expression of feelings in some places, such as the privacy of the home, the child's room, the backyard, or the car, they could have taught the child, "You do not give free vent to feelings in certain public places," without damaging or frustrating the child.

Can a two-year-old achieve control of any sort at all? Yes. Transparent as they are, even very little ones can learn to channel emotional energy in positive ways. Control may be partial or primitive. It will certainly not be sophisticated. But a beginning is a beginning—and an excellent start to a lifelong learning process. By the time the preschooler is ready for kindergarten, he or she should have a pretty good handle on when it's okay to express feelings and when you really ought to wait.

Remember that a tiny child's own feelings, when they run high, can frighten him or her. Remember also that the child's intense feelings are just as valid as any that you, yourself, experience.

Not infrequently, your child's displeasure or annoyance will be directed toward you. Edward Schatz would never have permitted his son, Ben, to get mad at him. I suggest Edward's attitude is unfair at the very least. Even worse, his attitude teaches Ben nothing about managing emotions in healthy ways. How might he handle a situation in which Ben as a preschooler (or as an adolescent, for that matter) became totally angry and frustrated with him—at anyone, in fact?

He could acknowledge the child's intense feelings without actually agreeing or condoning. "I can see you're really angry." Agree or not, acknowledgment is necessary. That validates the child's feelings. Validation is a wonderful and necessary boost to self-esteem and self-respect.

An excellent additional thought to convey is, "I get mad at people, too, sometimes." That forges an identity. The child is not alone or strange. Feelings such as these are universal. All men (represented by Daddy) and all women (represented by Mommy) have them too.

If apologies are in order, give them. Never fear that your child will see you as less than perfect or that you will lose face if you apologize. At this age, preschoolers see parents as perfect no matter what the parents do. You may be a mass murderer who reuses postage stamps (a federal offense), but you are tantamount to God in a preschooler's eyes. Apologizing does not dull that luster in any way, and it teaches profound lessons of honesty, humility, and godliness. Since your child considers you a demigod anyway, show the child as best you can how Jesus Christ, God Himself, treated others.

And finally, say "I love you."

I love you.

I love you.

(P.S. When Ben Schatz's grades did rise, with a sprinkling of B's among the C's, his dad was certain it was the badgering and browbeating that had shaped up the kid, though there was still room for plenty of improvement. In fact, Edward was pretty proud of himself for making Ben see the light. Grades were a big control issue between father and son, and father posted a small victory.

Ben knew it was no victory at all. True to the family's long history of not communicating, Ben didn't tell his dad the real reason his grades improved. Ben worked just hard enough to jack his grade point average above the minimum required of students joining the varsity chess team.)

Sexual Individuation

It started when Brian was about three and a half. He became extremely clingy toward Marsha, constantly under-foot and demanding of her attention. The little kid who used to amuse himself for long stretches at a time suddenly couldn't spend ten seconds alone. This was getting old fast.

At the same time, Brian became jealous of Tom. *Jealous* was the only word to describe it. When Tom sat next to Marsha on the sofa watching TV, Brian shoved in between them. When Tom arrived home from work and kissed her, Brian wedged between them, fussing. This, too, was getting old fast.

And it was perfectly normal. Somewhere during this preschool period, usually between the ages of three and a half and four and a half, a mysterious and special step in a child's individuation takes place. In boys, the complex of behaviors is called Oedipal, and in girls, it's the Electra complex. We aren't certain how it works, but we believe that very deep, below conscious level, this is the process that takes place:

1. Brian recognizes almost innately that Daddy and Mommy differ fundamentally. Since Brian's birth, Daddy has been All Men, the measure against whom all the men Brian will ever meet or be are compared, either consciously or below conscious level. Mommy is All Women. Same comparison.

2. Brian sees that Mommy and Daddy are united. This is marriage.

3. Brian wants to be united with Mommy, to be married. Understand that sexual significance is *never,* ever a

part of this process. We are talking about soul union here, not physical union. Brian becomes intensely jealous of All Men, Daddy, who actually holds the position of unity with Mommy that he yearns for.

4. Brian comes to realize that the union of Mommy and Daddy is solid. It will not be broken.

5. His yearning makes a subtle and, oh, so important shift. Brian wants to be united with a woman *like* Mommy. The visible aspects of the complex disappear and life returns to normal.

Down in this very deepest world below conscious level, Brian has made a profound discovery. He does not have to undertake the responsibility that union with Mommy/All Women would demand. Brian is free to be a little boy, the child, and receive the nurturing of both Mommy and Daddy. He has also come to realize the fundamental differences between men and women and identified himself as Daddy—as one of All Men.

Although the process is most obvious in boys, it occurs in girls also. Again, none of this goes on at the conscious level. Even if it did, the child would not be able to articulate its profundities.

Suffice it to say, this process works well only when Daddy and Mommy are comfortably united. What about Sara? Her mother, All Women, is not well united to All Men. As a result, Sara will not as comfortably understand at a primal level what men and women and unity are all about. She will learn later by observation of others, when her awareness of people outside her immediate circle sharpens. She will overcome, perhaps to a large degree, the experience she is missing as a preschooler. But frankly, the future lesson is simply not the same thing as the brief window of opportunity here, at this point in her young life.

The family unit is the child's primary social contact, but sooner or later, the child must come to terms with the whole big, wide world outside. Social development, as well as all the other fundamental concepts of life, takes a giant step forward in the preschooler.

5. WHAT ARE FRIENDS FOR?

SOCIAL DEVELOPMENT

There is always one moment in childhood
when the door opens and lets the future in.

GRAHAM GREENE, *The Power and the Glory*

H

e doesn't have a social life." Marsha watched her little Brian playing in the rice box. (When a sandbox is indoors, rice makes better sand than sand does; it doesn't get ground into the rug, it's not dusty, and it cleans up well, going back into the box easily when it's scattered.) "I bring him to play with other children his age and the only real interaction he has with them is fights over toys." Marsha waved her hand, frustrated. "Look at all the toys available! And he thinks he has to fight!"

At the moment, Brian was trying to make a blue block stay stacked on two red ones. Along came another two-year-old, Terry. Terry rammed his truck into Brian's pile of blocks, cackling with delight.

Terry's mother and Marsha both came out of their corners roaring. Terry was chastised for interfering; his mother was embarrassed. So, in a way, was Marsha. The only one unperturbed by the incident was Brian. He viewed Terry's action as just another possible solution to his problem.

The third year of life marks the first serious overture a child makes from the familiar setting of his or her home into the less familiar setting of the outside world. Granted, most children have probably had considerable experience with this already during their parents' forays into the outside world. However, during these trips to the park, the zoo, the grocery store, the visit to Santa at the mall, the child so far has been pretty much a passive participant.

For example, Brian loved to feed the pigeons popcorn. But his mommy directed every step of the process, including holding the bag for him. In encounters with human beings, Brian was always snugly sequestered under his mommy or daddy's wing. With adults, he remained close to his parents. Associations with small children were carefully supervised.

Brian's behavior in play groups was highly typical. He would conduct what's called "parallel" play. Although he was in the company of other children about his age, he played independently of them. Theirs was not a group endeavor of any sort. A toddler will stumble, step, or push his or her way over and across other children in order to reach a new toy as if the other children didn't even exist. As far as socialization is concerned, they don't.

Somewhere within this third year, we see a new behavior begin to emerge. Parallel play will continue. But in addition, children will attempt, and often succeed in, cooperative play. It takes two kids to make a seesaw work. By age four or five, the preschooler should be well on his or her way to developing peer friendships and to actually play *with* them instead of merely playing beside them.

This socialization does not necessarily start out in the world. The first steps happen in the home.

Helping Your Child Successfully Enter the Outside World

Of much importance are some of the seemingly routine daily interactions between parents and their young children. In fact, it happens that such simple tasks as helping set the table are the precursors to apparently unrelated skills such as reading and mathematics comprehension.

Let's use helping to set the table as an example. Sandi, mentioned in Chapter 3, stores her dishes not in a cabinet above the sink but in the lower cabinet, where her pre-schooler can reach them. Allowed to set the table, the tot carefully carries plates to the table one at a time. ("The manufacturer claims you can't break this stuff," said Sandi, "but my kid proved them wrong.") Next the child sets out the flatware, which also is stored in a lower drawer.

"When she first began performing this chore," Sandi reports, "we started every meal with a big flatware exchange immediately following grace; one person might have two or three forks, so he'd swap until we each had the correct complement of utensils."

Misdirected flatware was inconsequential. The child received lots and lots of praise. Now what did the little girl learn?

Proper table setting was the surface lesson. It did not "take" fully for another year or two, but the roots of it were there. More important, though, do you see the beginnings of counting and math? Four family members. Four settings. Four places. Three plates would not suffice; five were too many.

Language: A lot of verbal interaction took place as the child talked about the task; the mother talked, too, guiding at times, praising frequently, perhaps requesting a bread plate be added to the setting or sending out soup spoons as well. It was a real grown-up conversation.

The beginning of socialization: The child was serving others. She was serving Mommy by helping and serving the other family members by preparing the table for them.

By doing so she learned a profound lesson: At the tender age of two, this child was *useful and appreciated*. She mattered. She was important. She was noticed. She was praised. Heady, heady lessons from a task done, technically speaking, incorrectly.

By the age of four, the child was handling the task correctly and well. Competence became a victory of its own on another plane. "I can do it" and "I can do it correctly" are two separate skills, each of them deserving lavish praise.

A two-year-old thinks largely symbolically. A stick is as much a gun as a gun is, a block as much a truck as a truck is. The child is thinking about trucks, and any old symbol will do. This replacement and substitution lie at the heart of art and letters. Letters are symbols of sounds— a person who is reading is essentially listening to spoken words with eyes instead of ears. Written numerals are substitutes for the quantities they represent. The person viewing a painting or drawing sees infinitely more than a flat surface with marks. Words and numbers are powerful symbols of concepts. The incredible sophistication of the written language extends its roots clear down to here, to this preschool age, as the child learns fundamental lessons of substitution and alternative meaning.

Play: The best way you will prepare your child for life in the outside world is simply to encourage play. Remember, as your child performs an activity and explores the surrounding world, he or she is busily using all of the senses—sight, sound, taste, touch, and smell—even more than are most adults. None of these senses except touch is quite as well developed yet as it will be later. No matter. They suffice well. As you interact with your child, encourage them all. Figure 5.1 illustrates some of the advantages.

The ideal way to capitalize on this play is by spending time down on the floor with your child. The very presence and participation of Mommy or Daddy imbues play with importance. *This must be important. They are investing their time and interest in it.* The corollary also pertains: *They are with me; they love me.*

Somehow, it usually is easier for moms to get down and dirty. As a general rule (with many exceptions), mothers enjoy the process, the doing. Fathers tend to see a goal and hasten toward that goal rather than idly meandering about in the fields of random play. Small children are people of process, enjoying the doing rather than the end. Fathers may have to shift gears in order to fit into the child's mind-set. It's worth it.

Working parents, with a time crunch built into their hectic lives, must invest what time they can in this crucial play, picking bits and pieces of hours from here and there; most chores are less important priorities. The dog must be fed but the floors need not be waxed.

Often the time crunch can be minimized by allowing the child to participate in the adult's necessary work. Be forewarned that by permitting a child this age to help, you will effectively double your time spent on the project, but the long-term result will be worth the patience required.

Letting children help adults meshes well with another phase of this learning process, mimicry. Preschoolers ape what they see around them. For example, when my Matthew was small I got him a little rake and hoe. As I went about the yard weeding and cleaning up, so did he, churning the dirt here and there. By imitating me he established himself as a big person, doing adult things, and he worked off a lot of energy in a wholesome way.

PLAY ACTIVITIES AND HOW
THEY RELATE TO LATER SKILLS

Activity	Later Skill
Playing on a swing set challenges a child physically.	Leads to future reading/writing skills.
Playing with blocks, stacking, loading in a bucket or truck.	Leads to future math and science skills, size-weight-number concepts.
Play dress-up, pretend to be adults, learn small-muscle skills.	Writing skills, self-reliance, abstract concepts.
Play with puzzles and pictures. Learn sorting, classifying, and completion of a task.	Reading, writing, pegboards, math skills. Future study habits and self-esteem.
Drawing or scribbling on a paper. Learning to use symbols for objects and writing as a means of communication.	Reading and writing skills.
Art projects—cutting, coloring.	Reading, writing, and pasting skills, art concepts, creativity, imagination, painting.
Play with play dough, explore senses with objects and sounds, talking about outside world, seasonal changes, animals.	Helps with science and future logical thinking skills. Learning observation skills, cause-and-effect patterns.
Helping Mom or Dad in the kitchen, making a simple recipe, setting the table.	Leads to future math skills and forms a basis for self-esteem. Child learns a sense of pride in accomplishments and learns about dimensions, measurements, and sorting.

Activity	Later Skill
Reading a book with an adult, learns muscle coordination by turning pages and the left-to-right concept of reading.	Future reading and writing skills. Also language development. Listening and talking about a story, a child learns to notice details and express ideas. A child also learns about completion of a task by reading a book to its end.
Catch and throw balls. Blow bubbles and chase and pop them.	Future physical skills and science skills. A child learns hand-eye coordination and cause-and-effect relationships.
Imitating Mom or Dad in activity. When I bought my son, Matthew, a toy rake and other garden tools, he joined me in the garden. We could then admire together the fruits of our joint labors.	Leads to future science and math skills as well as sharpened physical coordination skills and social skills (two people accomplish more together as a team).
Playing with toys in a pool or a bathtub helps a child learn about cause and effect, and develop small motor skills, sorting objects by size, and learning about the concept of volume (by pouring water into one container or another).	Leads to future math and science skills as well as small-motor skills.
Playing doctor, grocery store, or post office, or another make-believe situation with Mom or Dad. A child learns concepts about the outside world. It's perfect to do this right after you've made a trip to such a place.	Helps a child learn future abstract thoughts and reasoning. Sharpens a child's social skills.

FIGURE 5.1

Will he ever be a gardener, amateur or professional? No one knows, least of all Matthew. Mimicry and play are important preparation for life and for socialization, but rarely are they job training. They're not intended to be. Matthew, now in middle childhood, is very good at weeding. Whether he ever pulls a weed as an adult matters not. His life and mine are the richer for our time together in the garden. That is enough. Remember:

Children of all ages spell love T-I-M-E

Socialization cannot be limited now to interaction with parents and siblings. It involves total strangers. It involves being more or less on one's own in a social situation. For most children, that opportunity comes with the first contacts at a day care facility or nursery school.

Socializing with Strangers

Nursery School or Early Preschool
Brian was obviously brilliant. Just look at him. Beaming with pride, Tom felt an immediate need to get Brian into an accelerated program commensurate with his superior potential. Marsha saw the opportunity to have a few hours a day to herself—and of course, she agreed with Tom's analysis of their son's potential.

When I talk about nursery schools I mean facilities for teaching the very young as opposed to facilities that see their primary function as day care. Some of these schools require intelligence testing as a prerequisite for admission. Need I mention that almost always, parental pride and parental self-image play a strong role here?

Be advised:

Indications of superior intelligence in a child this age do not equal superior intelligence or development.

Giftedness, quirkiness, talent, mental problems and mental acuity, sluggishness, or hyperactivity may not show up for years yet. A child this age is a mass of unidentified potential, and assigning labels such as *gifted* or *problem* is sheer foolishness. There are certain problems you should watch for: physical challenges such as hearing loss, visual problems, and physical reasons for reduced dexterity. Catching these problems early is important to seeing a good outcome in spite of them. Also watch for entitlement (that is, being dangerously spoiled), should it raise its ugly head.

If you're going to use a nursery school as an enrichment source—and they surely are—what do you look for? These suggestions pertain whether you're seeking a nursery school or day care center.

Lots of random play time

"But my child gets that at home!" you protest.

That's right, but even the most gifted child benefits from random play and interaction, more than from any structured school setting. Structure is nice. In later years it will be essential. Now, however, the child is using play to sort out life. Every child's sortings, so to speak, differ. Structured play does not allow for the many differences.

Lots of creative play items

Children of two are not yet into playthings such as Tinkertoys and Legos, the stuff older children use to express their creativity. By the age of five they are. Preschoolers exhibit a wide, wide range of interest and development. A well-furnished nursery school will have lots of toys with which to imagine situations—doll strollers, trucks and cars, toy grocery carts, and pull toys. The items will be too big to fit in little mouths, with no parts that come away easily. There will be things to climb on and dig in and lots of opportunity for active play. Wagons, trikes, and Big Wheels are nice.

Lots of supervision

The people operating the school should show a genuine interest in and affection for small children. They should know about the latest research and proven methods in their field and be prepared to deal comfortably with difficult children. They should be fully licensed, and their facility should be completely up to code. Six children for each adult is the maximum ratio you should see, and three to five kids per grown-up is better.

Facilities such as these should be considered adjuncts to the play a child engages in at home. At this age, a child is simply not prepared for a formal school setting in the same way as a five- or six-year-old is. Home is still where the action is centered.

Day Care

But home is not always an option. For single parents such as Shauna and Jenny, or for couples who must both work, day care becomes a necessity. And yet:

Full-time day care is not in the best interest of a child under the age of three.

A dilemma. Irresistible force meets immovable object. Now what?

From the viewpoint of the child's best interests, let's look at the usual options, listed in order of descending desirability:

1. Parent's alternate work arrangement
2. Single-adult care (preferably by a relative)
3. Consistent day care arrangement with high adult-to-children ratio
4. Custodial day care with low adult-to-children ratio
5. Inconsistent childcare arrangement

Let me take each one of these individually and discuss how you can make the most of these opportunities you have with your child.

Parent's Alternate Work Arrangement. Tom and Marsha Jasper used a variation of this option: Tom worked full-time and Marsha remained at home with Brian. Let's say that instead, when Brian arrived, Marsha had a good pay-ing job and Tom did not. After her maternity leave ended, Marsha would go back to work and Tom would remain at home to take over as primary caregiver.

This isn't a problem. Daddy can handle the task of childcare just as well as Mommy can. The only hitches involve ego. The parent who can successfully put himself or herself aside in favor of the child will do what is best for the child. And one parent as primary caregiver, assisted by the other parent when possible, is by far best.

Today's working world is changing as we speak. Such innovations as the fax machine, home computer, electronic mail, voice mail, and cellular telephone have made the traditional office far less necessary to successful business than it once was. Some people now have the option of spending the working day at work without leaving home. Such a system can be a mighty help during these first three years as your child is getting started.

One note of caution, however: You will find it difficult, perhaps impossible, to maintain the same level of work you did at the office when you're home and caring for your preschooler. You may wish to hire a baby-sitter for at least part of the day so you can have some uninterrupted time to work. Nap times are a blessing, but an older pre-schooler is probably outgrowing them.

A third variation on alternating work schedules is a part-time or more-than-part-time job for both parents. They can then shift schedules so that one parent or the other can be home with the child. An example that comes to my mind is a couple who live north of my home. He works for the state park system, and she is the curator of a museum associated with a college. Their two places of work are nearly forty miles apart, so they found a house about halfway between the two. She works a four- or five-day week depending upon the season, and he works three ten-hour days. Their schedules mesh in such a way that they have to put their two preschoolers into day care only one day each week and, during the off-season, not at all.

The downside, of course, is that they never have a weekend day together when neither is working. A schedule such as theirs is not set in stone forever and ever, but for the next few years, while their little ones are still so young, it is better for the children's sake than having weekends free.

Job-sharing is another option. With this arrangement,

two people perform one full-time job, such as teaching, by splitting the hours between them. Neither gets a full day's pay, but that half-day's pay can be the difference between making ends meet and failing to survive financially. If both persons involved in this job-sharing have little ones at home, the children would be in day care only a few hours per day. That is far superior to a long, protracted time away from home and family.

Single-Adult Care (Preferably by a Relative). If a child must be left with a baby-sitter, the little one is better off with the same caring adult every day. Moreover, a relative or close family friend is usually a better choice than a stranger. There is an important caveat here. The close relative must consider himself or herself a baby-sitter and not a surrogate parent.

In Jenny and Sara's case, Grandma looked forward to caring for Sara, ostensibly to help Jenny. In reality, Grandma could not conceive of her teenaged daughter being an adequate parent and wanted to take over the baby's development, shaping the child along the lines she had used on Jenny. In short: She had a hidden agenda.

Sara's grandma did not realize, herself, that she had a hidden agenda. Jenny did not fall in with the unspoken program, and her resistance to Grandma's strict ways and rigid views generated resentment and strife between the generations.

If you enter into such a childcare arrangement, I advise you to draw up an official written contract spelling out the terms of a baby-sitting agreement. You'll want to touch upon time off for vacations, what you will do if your child is sick, the procedure to be followed if the caregiver is sick, the payment terms, pick-up and drop-off times, who will take your child to nursery school if at all, and who will be involved in the nursery school's activities. You also may wish to consider a time limit that spells out, "This agreement will continue for six months, from _____ to _____" so that no one will feel obligated to continue the childcare if any of the adults feel burdened or uncomfortable.

A caring adult, even if unrelated, is better for a child this age than an institutional setting. What might you seek in an adult sitter? Look for someone who will play and interact with your child, who will talk a lot with your child, and who will not plunk your child down in front of a television all day. Make sure this person is someone you can depend upon every day. A major difficulty with this arrangement is illness in the sitter. When your sitter calls in sick, you are stuck, and you'll have to find a quick backup. Do whatever you can to avoid changing sitters. Continuity is very important.

Anna Quindlen, a syndicated columnist for the *New York Times*, made some astute observations on this topic on April 14, 1994, when she wrote in response to a Families and Work Institute study. The research claimed that perhaps a third or more of professional day care is inadequate. Ms. Quindlen pointed out that the quality of mothering (and by extension fathering) varies just as wildly, with some good moms, a lot of adequate ones, and a lot of abysmally poor ones. Unrealistically measuring day care against an ideal that even mothers cannot meet sets everyone up for failure.

The crux of the issue, however, is buried about two-thirds of the way through that column. "While the study of family day care showed that only about half the children were 'securely attached' to their caregiver, studies of attachment to mothers show, happily, a much higher number."

Attachment. There it is. A child securely attached to the parents is far, far ahead.

Consider what day care arrangement will help your preschooler best attach to the caregiver. Everything else is secondary.

Day Care with a High Adult-to-Children Ratio. The benefits of this kind of day care are consistency, dependability, and educational resources. Your child will be exposed to many different experiences, most of them supportive of socialization. This arrangement also lets you avoid the dreaded problem of the sick sitter.

If you use a commercial day care arrangement, minimize the hours your child spends there. A maximum of three or four hours daily is the goal to aim for. When choosing a facility, look for cleanliness, cheeriness, and a good adult-to-children ratio. Three adults for every ten to twelve children is a good ratio for an institutional setting. Try to use a facility with a low staff turnover. Not only does your child need the consistency of the same faces every day, a high turnover suggests discontent and poor conditions.

Day Care with a Low Adult-to-Children Ratio. This is one of the least preferable forms of childcare. In the best of circumstances, these institutions provide only custodial care for your child. These are the ones you hear the horror stories about. A friend told me of a situation in which two adults supervised twenty kids. I use the term *supervise* loosely. Aggressive acts by children toward other children went uncorrected. "I was horrified to think that most of these kids will grow up with this as their primary nurturing environment," my friend told me.

In this environment, a child does not have a single primary adult with whom to establish a relationship. That is as important as the lack of supervision.

Inconsistent Childcare. By far, the least preferable means of childcare is when the arrangement changes frequently. When baby-sitters are switched or the child migrates from day care to day care the lack of consistency keeps the child fearful and off balance. Socialization is retarded as the child struggles to establish relationships only to see them evaporate. Remember that relationships are even more important to a child than they are to us. We can survive on our own, by ourselves. A child cannot, and he or she knows it.

Assuring a healthy childcare arrangement is one good way to capitalize on this opportunity of introducing your child to the outside world. By and large, television is not.

Managing TV

Says a kindergarten teacher, "I'm getting something I never had before—kids with such stunted social and language skills that they're almost unmanageable. Almost exclusively, these kids are television and Nintendo freaks."

I questioned that preschoolers could be hooked on Nintendo, let alone become skilled in it. She assured me they can be.

Interaction with a video game is not by any stretch of the imagination interpersonal action. Preschoolers absolutely *must* have enormous doses of interaction with other people—living, breathing, thinking, talking people—parents first, other adults and family members second, and peers third. I cannot overemphasize the *must* in this statement.

Television gives no interaction at all. There is much

ado about how violent acts on television influence children. The evidence now is clear. Small children who see violent acts on television (this includes videos) react more violently than children who are denied that sort of thing. More than any other age, this age imitates. It imitates adults, other children, animals, images seen on the screen.

You see, small children do not view television the same way adults do. A child being told a story by an adult perceives the story. A child seeing that same story played out on television does not perceive the story. Apparently, the child perceives the different scenes and vignettes as being individual. The story may well escape the child. The images do not.

Does this mean television is innately bad? Of course not. Used judiciously and in *very small amounts*, it can entertain well. But it must never, ever be used as a substitute for interaction with other people. Understanding how the child grasps these dollops of the world is one important step in helping him or her grow. Understanding the progress of your child's social development is another.

Indicators of Social Development

The First Inclination of Actual
Thought Processes

"Sara, could you bring me a towel from the bathroom?" Jenny Lawton called. Jenny had dropped her towel in the sink, and now, with her head upside down under the faucet, she couldn't get another one.

A few minutes later, Sara was back at her mother's side. "I can't find it."

Jenny squeezed the water out of her hair. "It's in the cupboard next to the toilet."

Another minute passed. Sara returned. "I can't find it."

"Oh, for Pete's sake, Sara, they're right next to the toilet. I'll show you." Jenny twisted her hair on top of her head and walked to the bathroom, rivulets of unwelcome water running down her neck.

A battery of cupboards stood "next to the toilet"— one above the toilet and one long one on the adjacent wall. Another set of cupboards, beneath the sink, could also be called "next to the toilet" if you stretched the term.

Jennifer opened the long cabinet on the adjacent wall. "See, Sara? Here they are."

Eagerly, Sara pulled out the entire stack. The neatly folded towels landed on the floor in a heap. "Towel, Mommy," she informed Jenny exuberantly, and handed her a guest towel.

Sara Lawton's behavior in this story could have been misinterpreted by her mother as a plea for attention. In fact, at first it was, indeed, interpreted as such. Once Jenny got past her pique at having to pick up and refold towels, she realized it was not.

Sara was not successful when she looked for a towel in plain sight. She could explore cupboards, some of which she could not even reach, or she could come to her mother for help. Some children would search through the cupboards. It happened Sara did not.

Children in Sara's situation would have been thinking through the dilemma: *How best can I find a towel? (1) Look for it, or (2) Ask Mommy.* In scientific terms they would pose a hypothesis and then try to answer that hypothesis.

When Sara came to Mommy for help in fulfilling Mommy's request, she was tapping into the mother-child relationship. Yes, there it is again—relationship. But more importantly, she was thinking the problem through.

Creativity

During the preschool years we see the first attempts at creativity coming from our children. They are interested in drawing now; perhaps they want to sing songs for us or play with musical instruments or sounds.

An increased interest in playing with blocks is another indication of creativity. Kids this age love to build towers of all shapes and sizes, tear them down, and build some more.

When the playmate rammed Brian Jasper's pile of blocks, Brian saw it as no big loss. The tearing down was just as creative as the building, for both situations were part of the process. It's just as much fun watching the blocks fall as it is stacking them up.

At this age, children become interested in playacting or make-believe. Make-believe finds its full flower now in the preschool years, when all the world becomes a stage, literally.

Role-Playing

"Pretend I'm a cow and you're a tree," said Brian when they got back from a ride through the rural countryside.

"I'm a fireman!"

"I'm a lamp!"

"I'm Mommy!"

Role-playing is an important part of socialization. Through it the child explores the lives and identities of persons other than himself or herself. Remember that at this age, a horse is as much a person as Aunt Mary is. Children have not yet categorized the living world into subcategories only one of which is "actual human being." One little boy wore his Ninja Turtle pajamas to preschool. He was a turtle, you'd better believe.

Kids who play at being firefighters, doctors, Bugs Bunny, Princess Jasmine from the movie *Aladdin*, mommies, daddies, and so on are well-developing children exploring identity. Don't count on your child to be the next Stephen Spielberg. This vivid imagination is a common denominator of children approaching school age.

A good thing you can do for your child is simply to participate. You don't actually have to take the role of Elmer Fudd to your toddler's Bugs. Saying, "Where's that pesky wabbit?" as you peel potatoes for supper is sufficient to trigger the game.

You can enter play with a suggestion as simple as, "You be the doctor and I'll be the patient. Doctor, Doctor, I have a pain in my stomach." Your child will love it. Not the least of the pleasure is to reverse momentarily and safely the adult-child relationship. Suddenly the child is in charge, yet not with onerous responsibilities. I mentioned in a previous book a friend who stretched out on the sofa with his favorite beverage and let his preschool nurse bandage various appendages. The sum of his effort consisted of lying there, perhaps dozing, perhaps answering questions, perhaps accepting a plastic thermometer under his tongue. The results of his efforts are lasting a lifetime. His adult daughter, now with a baby of her own, still remembers those nursing sessions with fondness.

Should a younger sibling enter the household when your child is in this third season of life, the older child will probably regress and take the role of "baby." If you could not work out relationship kinks cognitively, could not think things through, isn't that what you would do? Play along. Your youngster is figuring out babies, and that's good.

Switching Perspectives

The ability to switch perspectives is an indicator of a mature, well-developing child. Children are intensely ego-centered during their first three years, and rightly so. Without that egocentrism they would be unable to build a personal identity. The ability to look at things from another person's viewpoint comes with maturity (and frankly, at times, not even then—just consider all the totally egocentric adults in the world).

Switching perspectives, in simple terms, means putting oneself in another's place. The child will not actually develop this well until much later. But its roots lie here, and you can set the groundwork for it. Obviously, a child approaching kindergarten age will respond better than a child just past two.

For starters, try shifting perspectives during playtime with your child. For example, let's say you are playing house with your four-year-old son and he is doing the cooking. You might ask him what each of the family members can see, hear, or smell. "Can Daddy smell what you're cooking?"

As the child snuggles in your lap following a story, you could ask, "What do you suppose the baby is seeing while she lies in her crib?"

Hypothetical perspectives are just as good. The two of you have built that fort or tower. "What would a tiny little person standing on top of this tower see? What would he be looking down upon? How would the room appear?"

Shift perspectives geographically, but only where the child can see the place in question. Your child is probably not quite up to remembering landmarks out of context. As you go out walking, ask your child what it would be like to be on the other side of the street.

"What if we were standing on top of the big water tank right there? What would we see from the top of that?"

Getting inside someone else's head is an intellectual exercise probably beyond a two-year-old's abilities. Try it, but don't expect a good response until the next year or so. "In this book we're reading, the hero is a spotted puppy. What do you suppose that puppy is thinking?"

"How would you feel if you were the little boy in that picture and the Cat in the Hat talked to you?"

I do not recommend encouraging this concept when your child is angry or upset. Not yet. The child isn't likely to want to hear, "How do you think your baby sister feels when you grab that toy away from her?" during a reprimand. Switching perspective is a game at this age, not a tool.

As a part of encouraging your child's social development, you can also introduce peers into his or her realm on a casual basis.

Friendship, Two-Year-Old Style

Early in their preschool years, children do not really have a capacity for friendship as we know it. Here, at the front end of social development, as the child has just begun to sort out at-home relationships, friendships with people outside the magic circle are still unexplored.

If the child could articulate feelings in that tiny head, he or she might think something along the lines of, *I have heard about friends. My parents (and older siblings) have friends. My parents say So-and-so is my friend. Therefore this child must be my friend.* "This child" is quite likely the little person your child met at the swing set three seconds ago.

Friendship at this age is as immediate and ephemeral as a friendship ever gets. The child is conscious of possessing a friend only so long as that friend is present physically. Out of sight, out of mind. Literally. Conversely, in sight, in mind.

This is why a preschooler can make a friend instantaneously—on a train ride, at the park, in a restaurant. Parents, who see friendship as a relationship built over time, tend to be taken aback by this cavalier approach.

Brian Jasper, accompanying his parents on an overnight trip, announced to Marsha that the three-year-old he had just met at the motel swimming pool was his friend.

"But how could he be your friend?" Marsha frowned. "You've just met him. After we leave in the morning you probably won't ever see him again."

Brian insisted with his usual adamancy, "He's my friend."

Brian didn't know the boy's name.

At this level of social awareness, the lad was, indeed, Brian's friend. Brian had taken the giant step of recognizing others his age. He was gracing this other lad with humanness and personhood. If only we could all do so with more sensitivity!

You can encourage this widened horizon in several ways.

- *Provide your child with a variety of playmates, if possible.* Although some will be more familiar than others— the children of family friends, for instance—all offer socialization lessons. In any play situation, one child may be dominant and the other submissive. Ideally, those roles should shift. Shifting children is usually the easiest way to achieve variety.

- *Supervise your child's play closely!* Children of the same age may be at vastly different stages of development. Some are barely ready to socialize, and others are ready to rule the world. Conflicts and power struggles must be monitored.
- *There's no need to overdo this social experience in the beginning.* By late preschool age, however, peer associations are absolutely essential.
- *Provide your child a combination of social interactions.* Arrange for your child to be with others this age, with other adults, with you alone, and by himself or herself. (That is, playing by himself or herself. You would never leave a child this age alone, of course.)
- *If the child appears fearful, back off.* Some children are much more shy than others. Go with his or her temperament. Be sure to introduce social situations, certainly, but do it gently and with the protection of a parent close at hand.

Helping Your Child Handle Fears of the Outside World

Balancing the need to feel secure against the very human need to meet and master challenges is a major challenge in itself. Your child's first venture into the complexities of the outside world is a necessary step and a scary one. You will make errors of judgment from time to time; resign yourself to that. Your goal is to make as few errors as possible, knowing that a child with good backup—parents who are there—is remarkably resilient.

Little Sara Lawton got hit with an enormous number

of new experiences when she and her mom accompanied Bob Charleston and his two boys to the circus. Jenny didn't think to regard the situation as being unusual or scary. She, herself, had gone to circuses and seen them on TV. She knew Bob. His boys were somewhat hyper but okay, and they were neat, friendly, open little guys. Sara had been to the zoo. That's the same thing almost, isn't it?

No it's not. If something appears different, even something that is in all major regards the same, that something *is* different. Two different zoos are different situations because they don't look the same. Two different houses are different for the same reason. With her sortie into the circus, Sara was entering a new and totally alien world.

Let's pick apart the new situation, particularly the social components. Note that Jenny's response to nearly every component is similar; support and encouragement.

• *Bob's boys.* Sara had met them during rehearsals, but that was in a different context. In that situation they were virtual strangers. In this one they were strangers indeed. They were active and bigger than she was. Normally rambunctious, the Terror of the Playground became an uncharacteristically shy, withdrawn little girl. It puzzled Jenny to no end.

Jenny's response was to address the boys in a friendly, cheerful manner, thereby putting Mommy's stamp of approval and safety upon them. Mommy liked them. It was safe for Sara to like them too. Mommy also provided support by allowing Sara to cling close. Particularly, Mommy did not chastise or ridicule Sara's fear.

Jenny didn't think about her response, but she knew that bold little Sara normally took control. Therefore, she realized Sara's fear must be real and definite. This wasn't so surprising; after all, the kid was only two. Bless her, Jenny allowed Sara her fear.

- *Bob*. Sara would go through stages periodically in which she shrank back from adults, even Grandpa at times. She happened to be going through one of those stages now.

Jenny's response would be about the same; treat Bob as a welcome companion, and allow Sara her reticence.

- *The surroundings*. This particular circus happened to perform the old-fashioned way, in a big tent. Barkers and souvenir stands were all brand-new, colorful, and over-whelming. In another tent, the menagerie housed zoo animals closer than Sara had ever been before. Sara took one look at the lion weaving back and forth in its cage and wheeled against Mommy's leg, clinging desperately.

"It's okay, Sara." Jenny picked her up. "We'll stay far enough away so he can't hurt you. Look at those beautiful eyes! They're yellow. I didn't know lions had yellow eyes. And his feet—look how his feet are huge and floppy, Sara, like yours when your sleepers are too big."

"Why don't we go over to the elephants? Would you kids like to ride on an elephant?" Bob led the way out to the hay-strewn pen where the elephants were tethered.

His two boys, Nate and Travis, yelled in unison, "Yeah!"

"Come on, Sara. Do you want a ride?" Bob extended his arms. "Want me to lift you up so you can see the elephants?"

"No," Sara said emphatically. She buried her head in Jenny's shoulder.

"Sara, what's the matter with you?" Jenny tried without success to peel her daughter loose. "You're acting silly. There's nothing to be afraid of." She shrugged toward

Bob. "You guys go ahead. Have a good time. I'll watch and heckle."

Bob grinned. "Yeah, sure. You grab the easy part." He hustled over to join his boys in line to ride the elephant.

Jenny watched them pay their money. She watched all three of them jog up the steps of an elevated kiosk and step across onto an elephant's back. Travis howled with glee and Nate cackled. You could hear their joy from clear over here, fifty feet away. Bob was grinning wide enough to insert a coat hanger.

And suddenly Jenny yearned to be there too. She hated having to stand on the sidelines holding a shy little kid while they were having a great time—a great time she could have had as well, had she not brought Sara. Before, Sara had always been ready for an adventure. If Jenny had known she'd act like this . . .

Jenny Lawton sighed heavily beneath her burden of motherhood. She rubbed Sara's little shoulder. "It's okay, Honey. Mommy's here, and Mommy isn't going to let anything happen to you."

Again, Jenny handled it right. She didn't push Sara beyond the limit the child was willing to go. She reassured the child.

• *The show.* With its noise, color, action, crowds clapping and aaah-ing, all in that strange tent, the show was a spectacle to behold. Sara ended up watching the entire circus on Jenny's lap.

Not a bad place to be when you're two.

Afterward, instead of frequenting the ice cream carts and stands at the circus, Bob and Jenny took Sara and the boys to the little dairy stand near Sara's familiar park. Sara had eaten a hundred vanilla cones here kneeling on these red plastic benches at these red plastic tables. It was her turf. And by now she was fairly comfortable with Bob and his boys.

She was home. It was a good ending for the day.

If Sara were three, the idea that the world is full of scary things would not be so overwhelming. She would have had more experience coping with the unknown. Her reactions might be similar but they would pass more quickly. Jenny's responses would be the same.

If Sara were four and showing fear, Jenny might be tempted to discount it. "Oh, come on, Sara. That's not scary." Yes, that certainly is scary, and Jenny's failure to validate Sara's fear would damage without helping.

Preschoolers cannot yet mask emotion. What you see is what you get. Now, a manipulative preschooler might overreact in some situations in order to gain attention, but not in scary situations. What is scary is too scary, literally, and nothing to mess with. If the child acts fearful, the child is fearful whether or not an adult sees a reason for the fear.

Meeting the Fears of This Age

Just as small children experience global guilt, in another sense they experience global fears. This preschool time is the monster-in-the-closet age. Because reason has not developed yet, highly unreasonable fears can be every bit as real as the actual lion Sara saw at the circus. Most important, *unreasonable fears cannot be countered with reason*.

Let us assume that, like Calvin and Hobbes, Brian develops the powerful conviction that a monster is hiding in his room, just waiting for Mommy and Daddy to leave him in the dark. How might Tom and Marsha handle it?

• *Assume the monster exists*. Tom and Marsha gave up on the tooth fairy years ago, about the time their wisdom teeth were extracted. But to a preschooler, an imaginary monster is a monster. Real. Genuine. Dangerous. To deny its existence would help nothing, anymore than denying the existence of death would prevent it from happening. On the other hand, the monsters of this age are passing phenomena. Tom and Marsha don't want to perpetuate them a minute longer than necessary.

• *Acknowledge the fear.* Acknowledge the child's fear without validating monsters:

"Wow, you're really scared!" or "I'm sorry you're so frightened."

• *Counter fear with facts.* Two facts matter to a child this age: (1) The object of your fear will not hurt you, and (2) You are not alone. Mommy and Daddy are nearby. You are protected. Of those two facts, the second is the one to emphasize. It builds relationship.

Now, there is a small window of opportunity, around the age of four, when counteractive measures, however illogical, work just fine. For example, my own son, Matthew, went through a stage when he feared giant bugs under the bed. In the plastic spray bottle Mommy used when ironing, we mixed up some Bug Be Gone—water and baking soda, as I recall, or something like that—and Matthew spritzed it under his bed. End of bugs. End of problem.

That sort of thing would not work at age three, when the child hasn't had enough life experience yet to know you can spray for bugs, or at age five, when reason and improved life awareness say, "You're nuts, Dad." Around age four, though, it's worth a try.

What do you not want to do, besides invalidate the child's fear by pooh-poohing it or denying it? Never imply that Mommy and Daddy are afraid too. There goes the child's only security out the window. And don't break routine—by taking the frightened child into your bed, for example. Teach the lesson: This is a fear, and we will deal with it. It will not control us.

Adults who know what fear is—rapidly approaching guard dogs, heavy traffic, the IRS—tend to underestimate small children's fears. That's an error. Children use fears to process their world and develop within themselves. The child who masters his or her fear of the bogeyman, with support of the parents, is learning a great deal about the world and about himself or herself. Fears are necessary and valuable. Don't dismiss them.

Although Sara experienced palpable fear, she could not articulate it. Some people, adults included, never develop the ability to describe or talk about strong emotions. It's out of the question for a two-year-old. An adult's, "Are you scared?" will be met with at best an eloquent nod.

Still, a major factor in your child's social development and successful overture into the outside world is the ability to communicate. In the next chapter, we'll examine your child's language development.

6. HOW NOW, BROWN COW?

LANGUAGE DEVELOPMENT

Every vital development in language
is a development of feeling as well.

THOMAS ELIOT, *Philip Massinger*

Sara Lawton!" Jenny frowned sternly. "Did you lick all the chocolate frosting off the cake I just made?"

Eyes as round as coffee-can lids, Sara wagged her head. "No, Mommy." Her denial might have carried a little more weight if her cheeks, chin, and hands weren't chocolate smeared.

"Ben Schatz!" Winona frowned sternly. "Did you eat those deviled eggs I made for your father's lunch?"

Ben shrugged helplessly on his way to the refrigerator. "Who? Me?"

Who me, indeed. Around Sara's age of two-plus, children master language to the extent that they have figured out a new aspect of it: Words mean what we want them to. Typically, verbosity flowers in the preschooler, but it is not mere vocabulary expansion. Children also learn to manipulate language, to do things with it, to exercise power with it.

Moralists would call it "learning how to lie," and Ben certainly was being deliberately misleading. But Sara was not—not in the same sense. She was not lying.

Sara spoke the words that conveyed the meaning she

wanted her mother to hear. So did Ben. Ben used them to avoid invective. Sara's motives ran deeper.

Your two-year-old fears those big, all-powerful adults, the demigods called Mommy and Daddy in particular. The child will tell you what he or she wants you to hear or what he or she thinks you want to hear. Anything, you see, to allay the displeasure of a powerful person. Sycophants do the same toward kings.

There is no such thing in a preschooler's heart and mind as telling the absolute truth. Truth is relative to the situation. Fantasy ranks equally with fact. The child is not trying to be devious in the way we accuse a politician or salesman of being devious or misleading—in the way Ben was. A child this age has no concept of fact versus fiction. That will come in a few years.

Remember that preschoolers employ fantasy to work out an understanding of how the world operates. Fantasy is absolutely real to them.

When you catch your child in an untruth you will certainly point out the difference between truth and fancy. That is how the child will learn eventually to discern between truth and untruth. The process of separating fact from fiction will require several years. It's not one of those the-light-bulb-goes-on revelations. But were Jenny to punish two-year-old Sara for a lie, that would be an injustice.

The Communicating Human Being

"Mommy! Fire truck!" Brian pointed wildly as he and Marsha drove home from the grocery store early one afternoon.

Marsha glanced around. She didn't hear any sirens.

She checked her rearview mirror. "Where, Brian? I don't see a fire engine."

"There!" Brian waved his arm toward the passenger side window. "Fire truck!"

Marsha saw a bright greenish-yellow phone company pickup with a yellow light flashing on top of the cab. "You mean that truck?"

"Fire truck!" Brian sat back with a confident nod.

Why would . . . Aha! "That's really smart, Brian! You're looking at the color. That pickup is the same color as a fire engine." Marsha would have extended the lesson to tell him the name of the color, but she had no idea what they call that emergency-vehicle greenish yellow. It wasn't quite chartreuse, yet it wasn't a clear yellow. She wanted Brian to get his primary colors down before he branched out into esoteric hues like fuchsia and puce.

Brian bobbed his head knowingly. "Fire truck!"

Vocabulary and Communication

During their third year, most children understand the majority of words and phrases they hear on a daily basis. Whereas the child's vocabulary during his or her second year is between fifty and a hundred words, the vocabulary of a child in the third year of life averages five hundred words or more. By age four or five, the kid is up to speed at near-adult level.

As I explained in the second book in this series, *My Toddler*, children comprehend far more words than they speak. A child who does not speak much or well probably still understands most of the language flying about his or her ears and nearly all of the language directed at him or her.

By two, the child should be constructing some simple

two-word sentences. "I want milk," might come out "Milk want," or a bare-bones "want" with a pointing finger. Some kids this age will be able to carry on small conversations like Brian and his mom did, and others will only be using the occasional word and/or sentence. By age three, English syntax—that is, the way words relate to each other in a phrase or sentence—will be pretty much ingrained. The child does not yet know a noun from a verb, but use of those parts of speech comes naturally and correctly. Only much later, in school, will the child learn the mechanics of the language learned so smoothly now.

Language mastery (or lack of it) at this stage of life says very little about the child's verbal prowess later. Please don't anxiously measure your child against others.

There are several things you can do to encourage maximum growth in linguistics.

• *Don't use baby talk, not even with a toddler.* The child benefits from hearing the mother tongue spoken correctly. Baby talk and the repetition of nonsense syllables is fine in an infant learning to babble. By the age of two-plus, a child doesn't want to be a baby (unless another baby has just entered the family, in which case the sudden desire to revert to babyisms will die soon).

• *Use correct grammar and pronunciation with your child.* Human beings are born to communicate. It's programmed in. Children want desperately to communicate, to express to others their feelings, needs, and desires. They want to share with others the wonderful things they find new each day. Children are sorting through all those new experiences, and sharpening verbal skills helps the sorting process because most cognitive thinking is based on language. There is no student of language more eager to learn clear, articulate speech than a preschooler.

In their pell-mell enthusiasm to master language, children will use whatever sentence construction and grammar that seems to work. Some of the combinations kids this age come up with can be quite humorous, with a certain arcane logic as you think about it. Some of the unique words, the strange constructions, the mispronunciations may persist as family traditions and lore throughout the child's life.

Consider a two-year-old's description for catsup: "Bop-bop." Every time she dipped french fries in catsup, she said, "Bop, bop" as the french fry bobbed up and down in the catsup. "Bop-bop" has since been adopted by her family to mean any dip or condiment. Incidentally, she's twenty-two years old now.

"But won't I be encouraging my child's baby talk and gibberish if I let her continue speaking these nonsensical words and phrases?" a mom asked.

Not at all. You don't erect a frame house by putting up four completed wooden walls. You set the studs, apply the siding, lay the insulation, put up wallboard . . . The child, with those clever constructions and misguided usages, is hard at work similarly building. The finished work, painted and perfect, has as its core the rough-cut lumber of a child's initial exploration into language.

Incidentally, may I recommend writing down immediately the unique words and cute phrases your child coins. As certain as you are that you will never forget them, jot them on a sheet of notebook paper in the back of the photo album anyway—just in case you forget. Trust me on this.

• *Relax, and let language be an adventure.* A friend of a friend wrinkled her nose when the friend used "pooh-pooh" in the child's presence to indicate feces. "You don't use those baby words, surely!" the friend of a friend fumed.

"So what *do* you call feces?" the friend asked.

"A B.M., of course."

Substituting a euphemism for a slightly more sophisticated euphemism isn't much progress. And being a hardnose about language construction and usage is no fun at all.

Are childish euphemisms such a bad thing? Of course not. Some alliterative euphemisms come in handy. "Pee-pee," for example, is the universal childism for urination. I have adult acquaintances who still say "ca-ca" in lieu of "dirty" or "soiled."

Should you correct your child's linguistic efforts? I would try very hard not to. Use good language yourself as an example. The good example is what the child needs most. Recast the child's communications in your own words to make sure you're getting the meaning right. Praise good communication, even if the language is technically faulty. Good speech will come. It will come.

• *Don't insist too early on the rote expressions of good manners, such as "please" and "thank you" unless the child hears them in common conversation around the house.* Early preschoolers will find it nigh unto impossible to remember the standard phrases of politeness unless the child hears them in normal use. Children turning three cannot remember abstractions such as the correct polite phrase to use when the phrase is divorced from the common currency of speech. "Please" and "thank you" and "excuse me" have nothing to do with communicating information. They are addenda, and as such are very difficult to remember on cue.

The child learns the language by hearing it. Hearing Mommy and Daddy use the phrases of courtesy makes using them a snap. Only then does the construction come naturally.

By the age of three or four, it is appropriate to expect "please" and "thank you" of the child. It is always appropriate to treat the child with the courtesy of using them. Polite speech tells the child he or she is a valued person with status as a human being and extends far beyond the useful device of being an example.

• *Analyze regression.* Brian enters a half-day nursery school and instantly forgets every phrase he used to speak. A child watches Baby Sister come home from the hospital and abandons her previously good potty habits. Exuberant Sara goes to her first circus and becomes shy, clinging, and uncertain.

Regression is a return to the "good old days." For a preschooler, the good old days are last week. The good old days are when life was simple and not much was expected of you. When you were a baby, before all this big-kid business, people doted on you and served you. If a new baby has entered the picture, just look at the intense attention and preferred treatment the little twerp gets!

Regression invariably produces a deterioration in language skills. That's natural. In fact, so is regression. It is a symptom of something else; finding that something else is the challenge.

Regression in a small child may indicate a source of stress—a new situation, a change from the familiar. The natural conservatism of small children resists any change. To identify stress sources, look at the child's world from the child's viewpoint. What is new? What has changed? Something as simple as a new color scheme in a freshly painted nursery could upset the child temporarily.

Is there fighting or hostility in the home? Friction

between Mom and Dad or between parents and children? Is Grandma moving in, and is everyone happy with the arrangement? What's going on emotionally that could tip a small child off balance?

Reducing the stress will alleviate the problem. Masking the stress source or trying to hide it from the child will not. A child knows the pulse of the home from birth or perhaps before. You'll not put much past a preschooler. It's best to work on the stress source.

Sometimes, of course, that is impossible. When a new baby comes into the home, you can't throw it out with the bathwater just to please an older sibling whose nose is bent out of shape. You can, though, be patient with the regression. It will pass, though perhaps not for a while, as the child finds a new comfort level.

Regression may also indicate simply that the child has been progressing very rapidly and it's time for a breather. Two steps forward and one step back, a maxim so often true of adults, is true of preschoolers as well. If this be the case, the child will literally catch up within himself or herself and continue forward, reversing the regression spontaneously and moving beyond.

The Mother Tongue As a Foreign Language

As you listen to your preschooler, much of what you hear will, quite frankly, grate upon your sensibilities. You will feel an overwhelming urge to correct, to improve. Resist that urge by thinking how you would communicate in a foreign country.

Let's say you're in Mexico, and the only Spanish you were exposed to was in high school. Even if you made all A's, you now find that your high school Spanish was not nearly enough. That soda pop you just drank has trickled through your system. You're in a plaza full of people. You see a vendor selling marlin tacos. You go up and ask, *"Donde estas bano?"* At this point, you will almost certainly prefer being directed to the rest room to hearing a lecture on the correct use of articles and feminine versus masculine nouns.

Similarly, your child wants to communicate, not hear lectures. When we flounder about in an unfamiliar language, we use improvisation—mixing English words with foreign words, mispronouncing, and using rudimentary grammar based on our own language. It's a rough-and-tumble system that brings knowing smiles to the faces of the natives as the goofy gringos try to find a rest room or a restaurant.

Your child uses the same tactics, mixing and matching what he or she knows to build something, anything, that will get the idea across.

Keeping in mind the variety of stumbling blocks you would scramble over if you were trying to make yourself understood in an alien world may help you find patience with your child's emerging language arts. Admittedly, it's frustrating for reasonably mature parents to deal with preschool language and philosophy. When you find yourself tearing your hair out, don't think you're a lousy parent or inadequate in some regard. A verbose preschooler can drive a saint nuts.

And yet there is a freshness and splendor to these speech attempts as well. Here is pure effort being put into pure communication untrammeled by the restrictions of grammar and pronunciation. Any extra time and attention you put into your child at this point will repay you a hundredfold later down the road. Admiring and praising your child's victories today builds for tomorrow.

And yes, there will come a day when you can sit across

from your child, both of you with your feet up, and discuss sublime abstractions of interest to you both.

But that's not now.

Encouraging Speech

In a study done in Canada, researchers found a strong correlation between the amount and type of parental involvement in conversation and later mental and social development in their child. Some of the parents' methods and attitudes bore particularly impressive fruit.

The study was reported in the July 26, 1993 *News Tribune*, published in Tacoma, Washington. The article said in play situations where the parents responded to their children and did not try to control what was said or played with—that is, reacted instead of acted—the children scored higher two years later in intelligence tests than did those children whose parents directed and controlled the conversations and playtimes. You are now astute enough about the small child's mind-set to recognize why. The child uses play to process life. When a parent directs the play, the child's topics are not being served as well and possibly not at all.

"Intensive interaction with a three-year-old?" Both Jenny and Marsha would be inclined to wrinkle their noses.

"Do you know," Marsha mused, "how much I yearn to eat lunch with someone who's not wearing a bib?"

Intensive interaction need not be onerous. I offer the following suggestions for ways to interact verbally with your youngster with the goal of improving his or her language skills:

1. Read aloud to your child

This is, far and away, the most important experience you share with your child. Picture Tom Jasper reading

"The Three Bears" to Brian. I mentioned, remember, that children instinctively fear those all-powerful adults. That fear must be eased. Brian snuggles into Daddy's lap, a warm, soft, safe harbor from the storms of life, about to embark on an immensely pleasant experience. What does that do to allay fear? Everything.

Brian is learning about maleness and femaleness now. Here is Daddy speaking in Papa Bear's gruff voice, and Mama Bear's medium voice and Baby Bear's falsetto. When Mommy reads that same passage the effect is totally different. The same, yet very different. Two voices, one love. Make no mistake, the lesson is not lost.

And then there is the story itself, a classic that millions of children have enjoyed. The story teaches lessons about politeness and the danger of entering others' homes unbidden.

Beyond the story there are the pictures. In nearly all of the good children's books being published today, the words join with the pictures to tell a story neither words nor pictures can convey alone. Good illustrations tell wonderful stories that the limited text never gets to. Some books, such as several of Peter Spier's works, tell stories with no words at all. Spend time exploring illustrations with your youngster.

"What's happening here? Oh, look! The artist has hidden a ladybug somewhere in every picture. Oops! I see it. Right there. Can you find one on this page? Look at that frowning man. How do you think he feels right now? He says, 'Look what we found in the park in the dark.' Oh dear, what *is* that thing? It's living in a big jar, see?"

And on and on. But don't dominate the conversation. A simple "Oh, look" with a pointing finger can get the child talking. Helping a child see illustrations will be of great service to the child later, when it comes time to discern the details of different letters.

Most important of all, this is Mommy or Daddy engaging in the reading session. You bet: relationship.

2. Hone your child's observational skills

Brian's favorite pastime, feeding pigeons in the park, offered a wealth of observations.

Marsha picked up a molted feather. "Brian, feel! Soft!" She tickled his hand with it (not his nose, please; let's keep potentially dirty things away from little eyes, mouths, and noses).

They threw a stone in the pond. Marsha remarked on the concentric circles drifting out.

"Is the pond water cold, Brian?"

Brian stuck his hand in to find out.

"Listen!" Marsha pointed overhead as the traffic helicopter passed, thumping rapid-fire.

Children enjoy what we call global observation. When they take in a scene they more or less take in the whole thing. Adults, in contrast, will focus on one aspect of the whole, quite frequently missing important objects elsewhere. This is why magicians can easily fool adults with an illusion that would never get past a globally observant kid.

Encourage that comprehensive observation, but also focus on individual elements of the whole—the color of a flower, the texture of bark, the strange bug hand-over-handing across grass blades.

Also, notice that Marsha was not limiting their experience to visual observation. Tactile experience, Brian's native element, also figured heavily.

Doing this with your child, incidentally, will sharpen

your own observational skills as well. Not a bad fringe benefit.

3. Talk with your child

And I mean really talk *with* him or her. Not *to*. Not *at*. *With*. The object is to promote the exchange of ideas, no matter how limited the exchange, or for that matter how limited the ideas. While you're driving in the car or while the child sits in the booster seat and you are making dinner or while the child is being bathed at bedtime, find little bits and pieces of time and capitalize upon them.

You'll not have much luck discussing past events with children this age. Your best bet is to talk about events in progress—current events in the strictest sense of the term, because a small child usually cannot articulate memories well. Even recent memories can't make it well into the speech.

General questions such as, "What did you do today at nursery school?" will be met with silence or confusion.

You can promote your child's ability to articulate memories by asking what lawyers would call "leading questions." Literally, this is putting words in the witness's mouth.

Example: Marsha and Brian, then two, just returned from a visit to the zoo.

MARSHA: Tell Daddy about the tapir, Brian.
BRIAN: Tapir.
MARSHA: Right. What did he do?
BRIAN: (silence)
MARSHA: Did he lick you?
BRIAN: My hand, my hand.
MARSHA: What did he do to your hand?
BRIAN: Tongue!

MARSHA: He licked you with that big, long tongue! Didn't that feel funny? He licked your hand through the fence, right?

Brian shows his hand to Daddy. It looks just like the other hand, and in fact has been washed twice since the incident.

Brian really did savor the occasion and it was tucked away in his memory. But at this age he could not easily retrieve it and reshape it as words. His mother coaching him through the process taught important skills.

4. Encourage your child to talk

"Must I? If I hear 'Why, Mommy?' and 'What's that, Mommy?' one more time I'll fly right out of my tree." Marsha had reached the end of her tolerance after a solid hour of monosyllabic questioning from Brian.

There is a limit, yes. But do try to stretch that limit as far as you can. The child isn't deliberately trying to drive you bonkers, though it seems so. A two- or three-year-old's curiosity is such that the child hungers to know the answer to "What?" and "Why?" *now*. A minute later the question and the answer may be forgotten. The child lives strictly in the now. The lessons, though, are not lost, the language lesson in particular.

Older siblings often think they ought to speak for the younger child, since the little kid doesn't do well yet. It's a power trip for the older child, of course, and kids don't get to have many of those. The practice doesn't do a thing for the little child, though, and retards his or her language development.

Discourage older children and adults from speaking for the little one. Ask leading questions. Be patient. Above all, listen. Don't rush and don't interrupt. Believe me, doing it the right way is absolutely maddening.

5. Listen

Communication is less than half speaking and more than half listening. So we are a nation of listeners, right? Hardly. The average adult perceives less than 30 percent of what he or she actually hears. People who make their living interrogating others, practicing psychology and psychiatry, interviewing people, or trying to trip people up, as lawyers in court might do, may reach 80 percent on the job. Off the job, we're about the same as everyone else. When it comes to listening to a preschooler . . . can percentages drop to negatives?

Listening to your child does perhaps more than anything else toward encouraging good language. Most of my work with troubled kids is nothing more than careful listening. I listen to body language, to tone of voice, to the words not spoken, and to the things expressed and the things not expressed.

The latter is not so important with a small child because small children are not able to deliberately abstain from expressing a thought. A child like Ben Schatz carefully calculates how much of his true thoughts he will divulge. A preschooler tells you what the child wants you to hear, but there is no picking and choosing among a number of mental images or concepts.

This means that when a small child speaks randomly (that is, not trying to sway you or allay some fear), you are hearing what is going on inside him or her. Your very act of listening places the imprint of importance upon the child's mental self, the child's deepest existence. Does the child realize this at a conscious level? I doubt it. But the effect is there at a primal level that will last the whole life long.

Learning to Listen

Let's assume you're not nearly as good at listening as you think you are, which would put you among the vast majority of people. I'll cast these suggestions as ways to improve listening to your small child, but they work for all listening.

- *Listen more than you speak.* This is hard for Mommy and Daddy, who have assumed the role of guide and counselor. Particularly at this age, however, your child does not need counsel so much as a willing ear.

The first step: *Simply keep quiet.* It's so hard to do!

The second: *Focus on what you are hearing.* That, too, is extremely difficult. As I listen to children and their parents in counseling, I am focusing intently on their comments and unspoken messages because that is my job. I am trying to see through the surface to the underlying problems. That will require my undivided attention and a career-full of skills. You do not have that spur to careful listening because listening to a toddler is probably not your career.

Ah, but yes it is. Parenting is, indeed, a career as important as any in the world. It is a full-time career whether or not you can afford to devote all your time to it. May I suggest you approach your child's conversations as if you were doing so professionally, as an analyst or lawyer. What would you, as a professional listener, be hearing? That attitude will help you focus immensely.

- *Don't interrupt or complete the child's thought.* Your thought may not be the child's thought at all. Again, restraint is immensely difficult. You want to hurry the child along, get to the end of the thought. You won't always be able to resist interrupting, but do your best.

• *Use listening body language.* Certain gestures and expressions indicate listening, and even very small children instinctively pick up on them.

Crossing your arms across your chest indicates displeasure or separation. The opposite would be to keep your hands at your side or behind you unless, of course, they are busy with some chore. If your hands are doing something while you talk, that is usually not perceived as being inattentive.

Maintain eye contact if possible. Either drop to the child's level or pick up the child to talk face to face. Both gestures are the same to a small child who is accustomed to being summarily scooped up.

Slightly exaggerate facial expressions of agreement, surprise, displeasure—whatever. Such mugging won't sit well with older children, but preschoolers buy it completely.

• *Acknowledge points and offer feedback.* What do I mean by feedback? Things like, "Oh, wow!" "That must have been exciting!" "I bet you must have been scared." "Then what happened?" Priming the pump, as it were.

To confirm you heard well, try repeating the gist of a tale back to your child. That's called reflective listening. We do it a lot in counseling. This is especially helpful for very small children who are still experimenting with words and phrases. They hear what they are thinking (one hopes) in clear speech.

It's also a good self-check for you. Are you really listening as you want to do? Reflective response will give you a clue.

• *Be considerate and courteous.* Does a two-year-old deserve courtesy? Every bit as much as an adult. A child of any age is a whole person deserving full personhood.

There are times in your day when you simply cannot devote your full attention to an enthusiastic motormouth. You can brush the child aside with a brusque, "Not now. Can't you see I'm [busy] [on the phone] [doing the income tax]?" Or you can give the child the sort of courtesy you would extend a neighbor or friend. You're not abrogating authority. You're still the boss, but the child is a person.

"I'm sorry, Sugar. I can't talk right now. I promise we'll talk [in a few minutes] [later] [shortly] [in a week or two] [when cows fly]." The time element in all those promises is about the same to a small child. A minute is an hour is a day. "Later" is what the child will hear. By the time *later* rolls around, the child will have forgotten the topic to have been discussed. The child's life will have revolved into some other part of the universe. At this age, talking about something else altogether is just as good for language development as is fruitlessly trying to recall the thwarted topic.

Language Problems

Serious speech difficulties can start to show up at this time. On the other hand, what appear to be serious speech difficulties during this initial phase of learning language may be actually no problem at all. How do you tell the difference? You usually don't. If you take a concern to a doctor or speech clinician and the professional assumes a wait-and-see attitude, rest comfortably in that.

The only problem you must jump on quickly is severe hearing loss. Now is when the child's concepts of language expression are forming. A case in point is Jenny's friend Shauna with her little Afton.

At age six months, Afton burbled as any baby does. But the babbling and cooing tapered off until, by age nine months, Afton was not vocalizing much at all. You see, a baby takes pleasure in making the noises. When the child could not hear her own vocalizations, there was no pleasure there and interest abated.

Physical Difficulties and Other Problems
Diminishing vocalization is a sign of a physical problem. To test for hearing, call to the child when you are out of sight. If the child is six months old or so, the head will twist and turn, the eyes seeking the origin of the voice. A sharp loud noise—a dog unexpectedly barking, for example—should elicit a startled reaction even in a newborn.

Shauna had her baby checked as soon as she noticed Afton was not responding well to sounds. She knew by the time Afton was six months old that the baby had less than 10 percent of normal hearing. Immediately, Shauna switched to learning sign language and using it on Afton. That's not a minute too early. Children from birth on will pick up on sign language as readily as sound. Children with normal hearing who are born to deaf parents can sign much, much sooner than they can gather their faculties for speech.

Although the child won't be speaking for a year, an infant is already developing the precursors to language skills. Language is growing inside the child long before the first word is uttered. By the age of two, Afton was signing fluently and her mother struggled to keep up. Signing did not come as easily for Shauna, a hearing person, as it did for Afton. Not only was it not Shauna's primary form of communication, she was learning it as an adult. Both points worked against her. It's a separate language, and the major windows to language mastery close by the time a person is grown.

Incidentally, Shauna used exact English rather than American sign language. By using exact English, she was paving the way for Afton to master reading and writing. Children learning American sign as a first language frequently have trouble reading and writing properly constructed sentences with all the bells and whistles (conjunctions, interrogatives, interjections, and such) because American sign language does not use them.

The main message: Catch any hearing problems as soon as possible and compensate. Seize the moment! There will never be another moment this good.

Hearing loss is not visible. Physical deformities such as cleft lip and cleft palate are, and you already know about such a thing if it is present. A child fighting a deformity may be slow to speak or unable to speak altogether. This does not mean language ability is slowing down. Continue to encourage language skills as if the child were speaking clearly. Substitute written or sign language if speaking is a problem. But do not neglect language at this age.

Autism usually shows itself during the preschool years. Persons who saw Dustin Hoffman in the film *Rainman* saw one form of autism out of many. Basically, autism makes itself known with major regression in language development along with a noticeable lack of response to other human beings and bizarre, unusual behavior—resistance, incoherence, intense attachment to inanimate objects.

Children with this condition are unable to initiate or sustain *any* kind of verbal communication. They lack interest in *any* social interactions, and they have an intense interest in small objects. They are especially stressed when anything in their environment changes.

Specific language impairment is a condition denoted by lots of other terms you may have heard—developmental aphasia, childhood aphasia, or infantile speech. It is neither childhood autism nor a severe neurological problem. And it's extremely rare, affecting roughly one child in a thousand. Children with this disorder have trouble remembering the names for familiar objects. They have unusually slow development of vocabulary and comprehension.

Stuttering

Stuttering and stammering are natural for small children who are struggling with a complex new skill. There are steps that will minimize stuttering now and thereby reduce the chance that it will persist beyond the age of five or six.

- *Show that you enjoy your child's communication.* If you are embarrassed or disappointed with the way your child speaks, rest assured the child will detect your discomfort and take less pleasure in speech for its own sake.
- *No pressure!* Never press a child to complete a sentence or thought. The child will eventually get where he or she wants to go. Don't push with too many questions too fast. Use simple ideas, words, sentences, and phrases in your own speech. Don't over-encourage talking. The child may simply not yet be ready. Not every two-year-old is a chatterbox, though nearly every four-year-old is.
- *Make your child feel loved and secure.* The more comfort-

ing and soothing your child's environment is, the less likely a speech problem will arise.

Slow to Talk

Permit me to reemphasize: At this age being slow to talk is not a problem so long as the child's hearing is normal or near normal. Many factors may account for children being slow to begin clear speaking.

A twin or closely spaced sibling may be absorbing enough of the parents' limited attention that the child's development is slower.

Gender stereotyping may slow up either the boy or the girl, depending upon your cultural background. In some countries, boys are more articulate at this age; in others the girls take the honors. In neither case is it the child's problem.

When older brothers or sisters leap in quickly to speak on the baby's behalf, the younger child does not have any urgent need to learn to speak.

In a day care situation in which there are not enough adults for the number of children, the child won't get enough verbal interaction during the day. Tiny children do not interact with each other well; they must have older speakers to bounce their beginners' skills off of.

The child may simply be too busy learning other skills. Children who for some reason have fallen behind in physical skills such as walking, climbing, or running will learn those skills first before spending energy on language. Learning any skill, language included, takes a lot of energy and attention. You may not believe this as you watch your small one dance on the ceiling à la Fred Astaire, but children have a finite supply of energy and will parcel it out.

The child comes from a bilingual family and is hearing

two languages. Not to worry. In fact, rejoice. A child learning two languages at once will learn both languages slower at first. That does not mean language skills are coming along slowly. Rather, they're whipping along faster than the monolingual child's; the kids are absorbing and sorting so much more. The child will master both in the fullness of time and be all the richer for it. Statistically speaking, your bilingual child will have the advantage later in life with better linguistic skills than most people.

Naughty Words

Ah, how adept children are at picking up on responses to their spoken efforts! If they say something that elicits a strong reaction from others, particularly a positive reaction, rest assured they will repeat the winning word or phrase. How do you combat naughty words? Stifle your reaction. There are those who laugh at a small child's innocent blasphemies. Others react with horror and sternness. The best route is simply to ignore it or casually mention, "That's not a word people are supposed to use." Then go on with life.

Children using disrespectful or pejorative terms are doing so in innocence. The small child who calls you "stinky" is not casting aspersions upon you. The child is experimenting with communication. A strong reaction works at cross purposes.

Very well. If you don't severely discipline naughty words, what *do* you discipline? Let's consider that next.

7. SHAPING THE HAPPY CHILD

DISCIPLINE

If there is anything that we wish
to change in the child, we should first examine it
and see whether it is not something
that could better be changed in ourselves.

CARL JUNG, *The Integration of the Personality*

*J*enny and Sara Lawton arrived at Jenny's parents' house after church on a warm day in May—Mother's Day.

"My, my, don't you look pretty!" Jenny's dad seemed to be more accepting of his grandchild now that she was talking. He picked Sara up. "Are we ready?"

"I think Sara should potty first." Grandma still smarted when she thought about Sara potty training easily a week after she left Grandma's.

"Sara, want to try?" Jenny watched Sara's face for the real answer as Sara shook her head.

Jenny smiled at her mom. "She's wearing disposable training pants, Mom. It'll be okay." She neglected to mention that it was the first time in months Sara had gone into training panties. She was out of them now, wearing "real kids" pants.

"Let's go." Jenny's dad held the door for his wife as Jenny transferred Sara's carseat to the back of her parents' car. Neither of her parents had ever mastered that carseat.

Her dad had chosen a restaurant a few miles out of town. Called Country Home, the place sat on three acres of pasture land framed by a white picket fence. While waiting for a table, guests could stroll among the willows, flower beds, and gift shop, and admire a charming lily pond.

Jenny's dad checked the status of their reservation while Jenny, her mom, and Sara walked down to the edge of the pond.

"Look at the iris." Jenny's mom pointed across the expanse of manicured green lawn to a line of gorgeous purple flowers.

Jenny nodded. It was, indeed, a beautiful setting. She looked back at Sara and gasped.

Sara stood ankle-deep in the pond, her black patent leather shoes and lacy white anklets hidden beneath the muddy water. Rivulets of brown ran down her arms. She held a handful of gooey mud in both hands and clapped enthusiastically. She cackled as mud splayed out with each clap of her chubby little hands. Her eyes shone with delight.

The Purposes of Discipline

What would you do?

Jenny was shocked, her mother livid.

What would the appropriate response be? Jenny and her mother, who still maintained a vested interest in her grandchild's discipline even though she was no longer the child's primary caregiver, would have no time to think or plan a strategy. This was hardly the time to ponder the purposes of discipline.

Children manage to break rules and offend parents in so many creative ways that discipline cannot be handled in a cookbook manner: "If such and so happens, do this." The parents of a preschooler must have a firm view of what discipline is for, just what discipline should be applied, and how it should be applied—before it's needed. When two parents are in the picture (whether together or separated), they should be in agreement on all those points.

Let's suspend the mud-spattering situation for a moment, something you cannot do in real life, while we explore the questions Jenny should have had answered before the occasion popped up. The first question is, "Why bother with discipline?"

Why *do* you want to discipline your child?

"Well, uh," you respond, "so the kid grows up right. So she's not wild," or "So he fits into society without killing somebody. Uh . . ."

Parents most often offer these major reasons for disciplining a small child. Some are more honest than others. Which are yours?

_____ 1. To minimize the incredible annoyance of a small child's demands, noise, opposition, and other behavior.

_____ 2. To shape the child into a law-abiding citizen; to give the child a strong, wholesome character.

_____ 3. To punish sin and error.

_____ 4. To obey God's admonition to raise up a child in the nurture of the Lord. To prevent the child from sinning.

_____ 5. To look good. A wild, undisciplined kid makes the parents look bad.

_____ 6. For love. Well-disciplined children are happier.

_____ 7. To promote self-discipline, which is necessary for survival.

_____ 8. To enforce the parents' position as head of the family.
_____ 9. To help my child be more Christlike.
_____ 10. To teach respect for persons and property.
_____ 11. Other.

These are not equally good reasons, but they are all equally valid. You can pretty well sort out for yourself which are good reasons for discipline and which are not. Frankly, the only ones I really have a problem with are numbers 5 and 8. Disciplining children so the parents can look good is always detrimental for children because only perfect children make a parent look good, and children cannot be perfect. Reason number 8, to solidify the parents' position, is nothing more than a power struggle, the most heartless, damaging reason for discipline that I can imagine. Does this ever exist in real life? It surely does, particularly where a stepparent, girlfriend, or boyfriend engages in a struggle with the child over who will prevail and win the greater share of the other parent's affection.

Moreover, all of the above reasons can be modified. Number 1, for example, has an excellent point. Children can, indeed, be a powerful annoyance. You can almost certainly remember vignettes of someone's small child running wild in the aisles of a grocery store or disrupting a wedding. Kids have to be housebroken, so to speak. The veneer of civilization does not come naturally. And yet, to punish a child for being a child is something else again. Parenthood brings with it a large reservoir of petty annoyances that must be forborne. It's not the child's fault he or she is a child.

Identify in your own mind, perhaps by filling in reason

number 11, exactly why you will be disciplining your child. Write it briefly in a sentence or two to cement it in your mind.

Here's why you should write it down: Discipline is useless if it has no clear purpose. In fact, it's less than useless; it's damaging. You need a guide for the future, a reason for what you will be doing for the next fifteen years. This is it, the purpose behind shaping your child.

Look at the written declaration of your purpose as you would the plans for building a shed. If you have no idea how big you want to make the shed or where you plan to put it or what you're going to make it out of, any efforts you make will be essentially wasted. Yes, discipline without purpose is that fruitless.

Discipline also needs a goal, an ultimate purpose, an end in sight. This is the deepest reason for administering discipline. I suggest that it ought to be to teach the child self-discipline—responsibility for himself or herself. Nothing will stand the child in better stead than to realize that he or she can make the decisions and the difference, controlling personal behavior in order to achieve a favorable outcome.

Related to that is the building of conscience. Conscience, by which we sort right from wrong, begins on the outside of a child. Whatever Mommy and Daddy say is wrong is wrong. By the age of six or seven, that good conscience has been internalized until a message from within has been planted: "It is wrong to . . ."

Discipline enforces the external conscience until the internal one comes to full flower, and then it corrects with appropriate measures the lapses that invariably occur.

Discipline: Teaching your child how to be responsible for his or her own behavior.

How do you use discipline to achieve the goal? What is appropriate in one situation will not be adequate for another. What, then, is appropriate?

The Methods of Discipline

When Sara Lawton and Brian Jasper were infants, their parents disciplined them by redirection. The parents could literally pick the children up and point them elsewhere. That Ghost of Discipline Past doesn't work anymore. The Ghost of Discipline Present requires a more varied approach.

In the end, experimentation and revision will probably yield the best results. No children are alike, and no child is the same from one day to the next. Methods and emphases must change to keep pace. Ben Schatz changed forty thousand times in his twelve years. So will Sara and Brian. As much of your child's preschool years consist of opportunity for exploration and horizon-expanding, so is discipline the parent's equivalent exploration. Jenny would change as a mother during her next twelve years. Edward and Winona Schatz didn't change nearly enough.

Let's look at how Jenny, and the Jaspers also, of course, might develop a program of varied and effective discipline. Several questions should be answered and thoughts identified. One of them is related to point of view.

Point of View
"Call me Ishmael." Thus begins the Herman Melville classic, *Moby Dick*.

"It was a dark and stormy night . . ." Edward Bulwer-Lytton began the book *Paul Clifford* with the immortal lines Snoopy later stole.

Edward Bulwer-Lytton employed an omniscient point of view in which he described to the reader everything that was going on everywhere and what everyone thought and said. In contrast, Melville told the story of the great white whale from the point of view of one person, from within the mind of an itinerant sailor. You saw the scenes and the story unfold through the eyes of one man (whom you suspected looked a lot like Richard Basehart).

Point of view is the perspective from which you look at a thing. How you view your child's behavior will bear greatly on how you react to it. In the incident described earlier at the Country Home restaurant, Jenny's mom saw Sara as being perversely naughty. Somehow Sara knew she wasn't supposed to wade into that pond and get wet and dirty like that. She was just doing it to be naughty, Grandma believed, because she didn't care about being a good girl and she liked being naughty.

Sara's grandma was looking at Sara's behavior from Grandma's perspective. Grandma's opinions and attitudes toward the child were already fully formed—let's even say they were set in concrete. Grandma then interpreted any behavior she saw as being just another illustration to support her preformed opinion.

Jenny looked at Sara and wondered if that greasy mud would ever come out of Sara's pretty little white dress. How could they go into a fancy restaurant with the child dripping? They were supposed to be celebrating Mother's Day, honoring Jenny's mother, and here poor little Sara was infuriating the woman.

Jenny saw Sara as uncannily knowing how to do the

wrong thing at the wrong time. Jenny didn't have problems like this when she and Sara were alone. It seemed as if entering Grandma's presence threw some sort of switch inside Sara. Jenny interpreted Sara's behavior as good-natured carelessness.

And what was Sara's point of view? *Her eyes shone with delight.* That says it. From Sara's point of view, this outing to the restaurant was turning out to be a whole lot more fun than you would expect. She played in the water at home. Why not play in the water here? At some superficial level she had picked up that her beautiful dress and cute little socks were special, but she didn't really think about them as something to protect. Small children do not protect anything.

A passing couple smiled; the woman wagged her head. As they continued on, she said, "Oh, don't I remember that age! Darling, do you remember when Benny was two and we took him to the—" The voice faded.

Another question must be answered: Whose needs are being met here?

The Underlying Needs
The surface needs are clear. Sara needed to be cleaned off. Grandma needed to bring her fury under control. Jenny needed some time to gather her wits enough to respond intelligently.

Below the surface the view gets pretty murky, like that pond. Grandma needed her grandchild to look good to the world. We deduce that by knowing that appearances meant a great deal to the woman. People's attitudes follow their interests. Your innermost needs will depend upon the things that are most important to you.

Jenny didn't care much about appearances; she never

had. She felt sorry for Sara because the little girl didn't have a daddy. Jenny also harbored a walloping dose of guilt for not marrying a man to be daddy to Sara. We deduce that from statements she made. Grandma could not see her own enslavement to outward appearances, but Jenny knew all about the guilt and pity. She wrestled with them daily. Both of these deep attitudes, one recognized and the other unrecognized, would affect the women's reaction to this unforeseen situation.

Sara's needs? They depend upon what Jenny checked off on that list of the purposes of discipline. Sara needed to learn eventually that you protect certain possessions, such as pretty dresses, and that you wear different garments for different occasions. This, you see, would all come under reason number 10, teaching respect for persons and property. Sara needed to learn that different behaviors are appropriate to different surroundings and situations. You don't do just anything anywhere. That's a variation on reason number 1, for although annoyance was not a factor in Jenny's life (it sure was in Grandma's!), the situation offered a strong element of running wild.

But . . .

Sara was not old enough to absorb those two lessons yet. She was not intellectually capable of keeping them in mind. She would learn the concepts over a course of time through repeated lessons. This was one of those lessons. But her learning curve was barely headed upward. It would be a couple of years before she could routinely remember to keep her clothes nice and not wade into other people's ponds without asking. By four it would be expected of her. Not now.

So would discipline be in order? And if so, what would the appropriate discipline be?

Figure 7.1 illustrates the typical responses you or I or Jenny might give a child like Sara and from whose point of view such responses would come.

Choosing a Course of Action

"Course of action," incidentally, could mean no action at all—a deliberate withholding of response.

Jenny had only moments to choose a course of action. She could not dwell on the considerations we've just explored. Her point of view, laden as it was with guilt and pity, would prompt her first reaction, what we would call the gut-level response. Grandma's certainly did.

But the first response is not always best; in fact, it rarely is because it depends not upon the situation per se but rather all the baggage being carried around below conscious level, where gut-level decisions are all made.

Jenny should step past her first response and try to see the scene from Sara's viewpoint. Was wrongdoing committed? That is, did Sara deliberately act in naughtiness? Look at the bright smile. No hangdog look, no guilty glance. Sara had no idea she was in error.

What's the best way to reach the ultimate goal of self-discipline? Mild correction would be appropriate, but certainly not punishment. Sara had things to learn and she would learn them through repeated lessons, of which this was one. But discipline in the usual sense would not teach those lessons.

Back to the scene:

Jenny gaped, dumbstruck for one moment too many. Furious, here came her mom. Grandma grabbed Sara's arm and yanked her out of the pond. She literally turned

RESPONSE	POINT OF VIEW	RESULT
Reprimand. Sara was wrong. Punish Sara.	Grandma's needs uppermost.	Resentment. Tears, anger. Child learns very little. Neither Sara nor Jenny will enjoy the dinner very much.
Laugh. See how much fun Sara is having. Recognize it's partly Jenny's fault because she diverted her attention.	Sara's needs uppermost.	Humor. Enjoyment. Clean up Sara and make the best of the balance of the afternoon. Dinner will be enjoyable if Grandma doesn't pout.
Comment on Sara's bright expression and also reprimand her for going in the pond without asking first. There is a safety consideration here; Sara cannot yet swim.	Both Mom and Sara's needs met.	Possibility for some tears, but not as much as under the first scenario. Sara may learn what she did was not exactly the best choice. However, dinner will be enjoyable for Sara and Jenny if Jenny is short on lecturing, long on encouragement.

FIGURE 7.1

the soggy little girl over her knee to give her the spanking of her young life. She swung her hand high . . .

And for the first time in her life, ever, Jenny physically and totally opposed her mother. She managed to reach the two of them in time to grab her mom's wrist and stop her.

"I'll handle it, Mom." Jenny studied her mother's startled eyes and felt her own grow hot. "She's my daughter. I'll handle it."

Jenny scooped Sara up before her mother could mount an effective barrage of argument, the way she so often did, and rapidly carried the tot off to the rest room.

Jenny commenced a running narrative to keep her own emotions from spilling. "Grandma really scared you by pulling you out of the water like that. I see how scared you are. Hey, Sugar, you know you mustn't go into water without me! You never, ever go in water unless I'm with you!" Jenny knew she was with Sara, technically speaking, but she didn't dwell on that. She felt bad enough already.

She pushed open the women's rest room door and sat Sara on the counter by the sink. "Look at the mess! You have to learn to be careful when you're wearing pretty things. You want them to stay nice."

"Pee-pee, Mommy."

Jenny abandoned her feeble attempts at washing off mud and set Sara on the toilet, holding her carefully. She heard the welcome tinkle. "Sara, that's a good girl! That's such a good girl, to tell Mommy and pee-pee in the toilet! I'm proud of you, Sugar!" It took her another ten minutes to get Sara looking halfway decent. She didn't bother with a bib to protect her dress when they sat down to eat. "What can she do to it that hasn't been done?"

Grandma had acted from her own inner need and her underlying attitude that Sara took pernicious delight in bad behavior. Those strangers noticing and commenting didn't help a bit. Had Jenny's feelings of guilt and pity not run so deep, she might have backed off and let her mother take over the discipline this time, as she had done so often in the past. But Jenny was now nearly three years older than she had been when Sara was born, and she had been on her own for some months. Jenny had grown in resolve and in patience.

Jenny's guilt and pity actually served her this time, but it was more or less by chance. The next time those emotions might blind her to the correct response, perhaps letting her go easy with Sara in a situation requiring a strong disciplinary response.

The process, then, is:

- *Acknowledge the first response but don't carry it out.*
- *Consider the child's point of view in this situation.*
- *Modify a response that will best serve the goals of discipline and teach the child the lesson the situation offers.* (And assume every situation of inappropriate behavior offers a lesson of some sort.)

Notice that this method produces change in the child, as should all good discipline, but it also calls for change in the parent. That's not easy, shifting your point of view when you're probably madder than hops or embarrassed or both. But then, who promised it *would* be easy?

Knowing the reason a child does something helps immensely in tailoring an appropriate correction or disciplinary measure.

Why Do Kids Misbehave?

Misbehavior—I like the term *inappropriate behavior* much better—is any action that creates a need for correction or discipline. Kids do a lot of crazy and downright stupid things for a variety of reasons, but the reasons can be lumped into five basic, underlying ones. Some do not come into play until the child is older.

1. For No Apparent Reason At All

Why dump the goldfish, bowl and all, into the clothes hamper? Why lob a drinking glass in a great arc up into the sink to hear it shatter? Why hide the car keys? Sara did all those things one afternoon while her grandma was baby-sitting her. She was punished for all three behaviors. She had no idea why or what she had done wrong other than make Grandma angry. But then, Sara had given up trying to figure out why Grandma got angry. It happened at seemingly random times for myriad reasons. After all, Sara could see no connection between the fish, the glass, and the keys.

Small children almost never do things randomly or for no reason. However, their convoluted reasoning in some cases would baffle us even if they could articulate their motives, which they cannot. We chalk them off as random because we cannot understand them.

Related to these are simple acts of carelessness and ignorance. Sara may have known at some level that a glass can break, but it never occurred to her to set it down carefully. Grandpa and Grandma put their glass in the sink. So did Sara. Small children still do not grasp consequences well. It will come with time. Until then, inappropriate behavior will abound.

The response: Firm correction short of punishment. Grandma might pick Sara up and show her the broken glass. "See? It broke. Now we can't drink out of it anymore. Be careful with glasses! Treat them gently."

Grandma might be justified in being cross and sharp regarding the goldfish. Fortunately, Grandma saved the situation by retrieving the bowl and fish before the fish flipped its last flop. As for the keys, Grandma scolded and punished Sara but still Sara refused to divulge their whereabouts. Grandma was certain Sara was being very bad and stubborn. Sara was certain she could not remember where she had left them, but she was not so certain she would have told Grandma even if she could remember. The ongoing power struggle between those two strong personalities was nowhere near resolved. And in this case Sara absolutely held the keys of power, literally and figuratively.

2. To Garner Attention

Brian Jasper knew he wasn't supposed to bug Dumkopf, the Jaspers' weimaraner. He'd been corrected numerous times. But here was a patio full of Sunday-afternoon guests, and no one was paying attention to Brian. He grabbed Dum's ear and yanked repeatedly. The dog yelped, Dum had a piercing voice when he was really surprised and goaded. Suddenly everyone was looking at Brian.

To a youngster who feels neglected at the moment, negative attention is attention, all the same. Children, all children, want desperately to be the center, to belong, to be noticed. Brian was in no way neglected; Marsha gave him much time in the day, and Tom gave him much time in the evening and weekends. But to a child, 100 percent attention is still not quite enough. Tom and Marsha's attentions had been diverted long enough. Brian acted.

The response: Minimize the attention garnered by undesir-

able behavior. That is, no payback. Respond lavishly to good behavior.

Marsha had a double problem here involving kindness to animals and safety. Were Brian to tweak the ear of the neighbors' intolerant rottweiler, he could lose his face. Few dogs were as patient as Dum. Besides, she and Tom strongly opposed cruelty to animals.

She snatched Brian up and carried him briskly inside, away from the public eye. She rarely used physical punishment, but Brian got a swat and she explained clearly why: You *never* hurt animals or other people. Never. That was very wrong. She would not have used a swat for most other offenses. Because she and Tom were so reluctant to spank, her action now startled and frightened Brian more than hurt him.

Here, Marsha was acting precipitately on her first impulse, to prevent cruelty. In the case of Grandma versus Sara, the first response was not appropriate. In this case, it was all right for the situation. Marsha still should have taken a deep breath, stalled on her first response, and considered a second choice. In this case the second choice may well have been the first one. Still, it would be better considered. Whether or not Brian knew what he was doing (he did), he must know that such behavior is never tolerated.

A word here on time-outs, which seem to have become the preferred punishment of the nineties. And in some instances they can be very effective. Essentially, you lift the child out of the situation causing the problem and isolate him or her. This is the modern version of the old sit-in-a-corner-until-I-say-you-can-come-out ploy. It may not be a corner (most corners today are full of furniture). It may just be the sofa or a chair, the child's room, or a stool in the kitchen. For kids garnering attention, it thwarts the intent of their ploy. Removing a child from attention shows him or her that acting in a certain way does not get the desired response.

Time-outs are good to quell incidents of fighting and squabbling. It pries the kids apart and allows both of them to cool off.

The method, though, can easily be overused to the point of becoming ineffective. Physically forcing your child into a time-out can be perceived by your child as an aggressive act, since you're using your size and strength to overpower him or her. Be prepared for that.

Ideally, children can learn to use time-outs voluntarily as a method to gain control over their feelings. This is not something you can teach children. They will learn by imitation if you, the parent, do it yourself. When your nerves are rubbed to the point where you're afraid you'll do or say something you might regret later, remove yourself from the event and take a breather.

It will come as a surprise to the child at first when you say, "Mommy has to take a time-out right now. I'll be right back when I'm not so mad." You don't leave the child's physical presence, of course, or curtail the child's supervision. You sit aside, open a can of diet soda, and take deep breaths.

Marsha and Tom already took another big step in minimizing attention-getting behavior; they made a conscious effort to praise Brian's good behaviors.

3. To Gain Power or Test the Reigning Authority

Shauna's Afton knew Mommy was the boss, but once in a while she just could not resist making sure she knew.

Shauna flipped a rubber band at Afton to catch the child's attention. She signed, "No, Afton. Stay away from the TV set."

Afton eyed Mommy. That was Shauna's first clue. Afton had a calculating look on her face. With a sigh, Shauna put down her book and got up. She knew what was coming. Afton turned away and reached for the shiny tuner knob. You see, Afton already knew that as long as she didn't look at Mommy, she couldn't receive a "no-no" message.

Mommy crossed the room and signed "No-no!" right in Afton's face. The little arm dropped to Afton's side. A dimple dented the little cheek, the visible sign of a suppressed smile. *Smirk,* Shauna would call it.

Shauna stepped back. The hand went for the knob again.

Testing is especially big with children aged one and a half to about two and a half as they wrestle with separation and individuation. And small children have an uncanny ability to know what they can control—to pick the ground they will fight on. It's good military strategy; it drives parents nuts.

Afton was older than that. She was reverting. Afton's obvious attempt to test Mommy was both blatant and primitive, the kind of thing you'd expect of a smaller child. World-class testing and power plays will involve sleeping, eating, or potty training—things over which the child exercises the final say.

The response: The gentlest response needed to ensure the child's safety and compliance. Avoid making a battleground of the big areas of power and control.

In the situation above, since Afton was reverting to babyish behavior, so could Shauna. She picked up Afton and wagged her head wearily. "Now, Button," she signed, "you know better than that." By that she indicated she was on to Afton's ploy. "Let's get a bath and try out the new boat Jenny bought you." Diversion. That's how you handle very small children.

It worked only because Afton had no opportunity to return to the tantalizing knob or to the power play it represented. Shauna had won, but she won without confrontation such as spanking or scolding. Shauna, incidentally, was very proud that she could sign one-handed while holding Afton in the other; many signs require both hands for completion.

A general rule for minimizing inappropriate behavior for control reasons is to create an environment where power struggles will be minimal. Essentially, the parent does this by relinquishing a measure of control. Make situations like eating, sleeping, and potty training no big deal, and a good opportunity for the child to use these areas as control issues will not present itself.

Tom and Marsha minimized control issues by giving Brian areas of control. For example, allowed to choose his own clothes each morning, he occasionally wore shorts in the winter. Marsha would not say, "You can't wear those. Wear corduroy overalls, Brian." She simply waited until he got cold and suggested, "If you go dig out a pair of overalls, your legs will probably feel warmer."

4. To Take Revenge

Most children between two and four have not progressed to this stage of misbehavior unless they've been subjected to intense and constant physical or emotional punishment. I mention it here only so you can be on the lookout for it as your child becomes more sophisticated.

There are, indeed, children who lash out to get back at someone, and it may well be someone other than the person who actually hurt them. As children experience global guilt—feeling they are personally responsible for all the bad in the world—so are they lax about assigning responsibility for pain to specific others. Anyone handy is the person who gets the brunt of a frustrated, angry child's antisocial behavior.

The response: Physical punishment as a means of discipline is largely ineffective. It's just another instance of hurting. Read the child: Hostile mannerisms, sullenness, angry expressions and gestures, and yelling or talking back indicate resentment. Why? How would you feel if you were in the child's shoes?

Knowing what you know (or thinking you know) about the child's attitude, how can your ultimate goals of discipline (which, remember, you have already worked out in advance) be achieved best? You may find success with creative approaches such as restitution, time-out, alternative activity, chores, or some unusual assignment.

5. Because the Child Feels Inadequate

Again, you're not going to find this reason very often in preschoolers. They have not been jaded enough by life to give up hoping things will go their way. Ben Schatz, at twelve, had reached this stage. Consider it a possibility once the child reaches six or seven.

Basically, we have been talking about negative behavior and negative consequences to that behavior. That's only half of true discipline. Real discipline, the shaping of a child's conscience, involves positive action as well. Positive discipline is a new buzzword in child psychology today. It means parenting from an active stance—avoiding problems before they occur and encouraging appropriate behavior.

Positive Discipline

"Hey, Brian! Catch!" From out at the end of the yard, Tom lofted the glow-in-the-dark Frisbee. The sun had melted out of sight half an hour ago; like a blue-green spaceship, the Frisbee arced through the purple sky and skidded into the grass at Brian's feet. Cackling, Brian snatched it up and flung it. The disk dropped to the grass at his feet.

Tom had anticipated a singular lack of success on Brian's part. He stepped in close, and Brian handed him the Frisbee. Tom looked at his watch. "Oh, good! We have time for one more throw!" He jogged out and sent the Frisbee particularly high. Brian had nearly forgotten about it by the time it scudded into the flower bed beside him.

Tom scooped him up. "Story time. I love story time."

"No, bath!" Brian corrected.

"Oh yeah. Bath. Let's see if Mommy has the water run."

She did. Tom gave Brian a rather perfunctory bath (they were actually running somewhat behind schedule) and slipped his nighttime T-shirt over his head. They settled into the rocker in Brian's room for the story of Brian's choice. Brian held the book and turned the pages as Tom read. Now and then they'd discuss a picture. Mommy brought in a glass of warm milk for Brian—a very small glass they used only at bedtime.

Brian brushed his teeth as Daddy supervised, and Daddy tucked him in. Another day had ended.

In a larger sense, that whole sequence of activity was an exercise in positive discipline.

Negative discipline is the punitive form of discipline with which most of us are familiar. Spanking, forced time-outs, reprimands, yelling, or physical restraint all carry a negative element. Negative discipline seems quick and easy, but it is usually effective only in the short term. It stops the immediate behavior problem, but it rarely teaches the child how to act in the future.

Lest it seem I am giving negative discipline a black mark, let me add that it does have its place. When immediate and strong enforcement of a rule is needed, negative discipline will do it for you. I am thinking now of cardinal safety rules, such as running out into the street or playing with matches or electrical cords. In such cases, the negative discipline, if handled promptly and with the appropriate verbal admonition, startles the child into blotting up the lesson. "Boy, I don't mess with that electrical cord or else!" The more sparingly it is used, however, the more effective negative discipline will be when it is used.

Just the opposite, positive discipline provides long-term results and is best used lavishly. There are several specific ways to exercise positive discipline. Try them all. Different ways work differently with different personality types. Read your child and weigh the results as you work with these different ways. Remember that any discipline, positive or negative, will change as your child grows and changes.

Anticipate and Avoid Problems with Your Child

A lot of what little kids do cannot be anticipated. Neither Jenny nor her mom thought Sara would choose that moment to test the waters. In the adults' mind-set, you just don't wade into a pond in your good shoes and fancy socks. The preschool mind-set doesn't have a problem with it. So when I mention these suggestions, take them with a grain of salt. You cannot anticipate everything. There will be days you can't anticipate anything.

Prepare Your Child for What's Coming

Jenny Lawton could say, "Sara, we're going to take Grandma to a nice restaurant. We're going to wear our pretty church clothes. We want to stay nice and clean so we will look pretty in the restaurant."

Then she might cover as many other bases as she can think of. "We might have to sit still for a while until our dinner comes. Should we take along some crayons and paper so we can draw?"

I seriously doubt this would have stopped Sara from going into the pond. Jenny could hedge her bet by repeating these admonitions several times, including as they were getting out of the car at the Country Home. Sara would have had some knowledge of what was expected of her for the afternoon, but such knowledge flees easily.

Try to voice expectations appropriate to your child's age. Jenny could not realistically expect a two- or three-year-old to sit still during a drawn-out, leisurely dinner, especially not Sara, who was hyper anyway (although her grandmother did expect just that). The average attention span of a three-year-old is five to ten minutes. Jenny would have to be prepared to walk around with Sara and find ways to keep her entertained during dinner. By the age of four, Sara would be able to handle assignments of that sort better.

When Tom Jasper played with his son, he issued a cheery warning that they would be going inside *before* they finished Frisbee throwing. Preparation. Also note the positive way he phrased it: "Oh, good! We have time . . ."

Maintain Routine

When Tom suggested the next step was story time, Brian corrected him. Bath, then story. Small children crave routine. Brian knew the sequence of bedtime events and was loathe to vary it. Regular occurrences in regular progressions maintain their sense of security and safety. The big, new world out there may be scary, but home is predictable and secure.

It's rather like the Percherons that trot around the circus ring as trick riders perform dazzling feats upon their broad backs. The rider who performs a back flip or leap, leaving the horse's surface completely, has to know exactly where that horse will be when he or she comes down. Any variation on the speed or gait would put the horse somewhere other than directly under the rider. Thus, the horses are trained to jog in a constant rhythm. The tent may fall down and the circus blow away. In the aftermath, those horses will still be in the ring, jogging in rhythm.

Kids would understand that.

Avoid Nagging

Cajoling, haranguing, repeating an order over and over—you know what nagging is. Nagging immediately puts most children on the defensive. It probably does you as well. How do *you* respond to a nagger except by resisting? Same with kids.

Minimize nagging by thinking of positive ways to phrase your directions and, if necessary, rephrase them. I suggest that during these months as your child completes separation and individuation that you avoid statements beginning with *you* or in which the you is understood. A direct command invites direct resistance. Requests rather than commands present less opportunity for disobedience. Compare:

"Pick up your blocks. It's dinnertime." with:

"As soon as you pick up your blocks, you can help Daddy put the tacos together while I build the enchiladas."

Quite possibly about now the child will decide to help with enchiladas rather than the assigned task, tacos. Again, the child is asserting independence. The response would be, "Well, okay, if you really want to, as soon as the blocks are in their bag."

Keep It Simple

An acquaintance, a young man recently married, was running down to the store for his bride. She asked him to bring back four items.

"Whoa." He stopped in the doorway. "Which three do you want? I can only remember three."

A few days later he found a memo pad and pencil on his pillow. But his point is well taken. People can remember only a certain small number of things, be they items on a list or things to do. Some people can remember more than others can. With a small child, that certain small number is one.

One simple instruction. One thing to do. One day at a time. If your request contains more than one step, ask compliance on each step individually.

"Put away your blocks and get your toys out of the den" often won't work. That's two things to keep track of. The child is as likely to remember the second as the first and come to the kitchen to help while the blocks remain strewed about.

Use the Child's Name

This first year of the preschool season is particularly separation and individuation time. Using the child's name both personalizes your comments and separates the child from all others. It's an excellent device to use anytime, though it works especially well now.

Phrase Directions in the Affirmative

Avoiding "no" and "don't" and "mustn't" is positive discipline at its best. The phrasing becomes encouraging rather than accusatory, neutral rather than hostile. The message of correction comes through without the invitation to resistance.

This would never happen, of course, but let's say your son, Alex, has just dumped the peas and chopped chicken from his plate onto the floor. Now he is hanging over the arm of his high chair looking down at it.

Instead of "Alex, no! Bad boy! You mustn't spill your food!" try "Food is for eating," or "Wasting food is wrong," or "We keep food on our plates."

If controlling your own mood is a problem, feel free to go creative. Using irony, sarcasm, or humor, even if you are the only one who gets the meaning, can benefit you. You need the positive interplay as much as your child does. How about a laconic, "Done with our meal, are we?" Or, "That's one way to tell me you want down, but I don't think much of it. Next time, just tell me, all right?" Or simply, with just the right morsel of impatience, say, "Oh, come on, Alex."

The all-too-human tendency to bristle at negatives is nowhere more evident than it is in small children. They don't analyze sentences looking for things to object to, certainly, but their reactions, all gut-level and unreasoned, respond to negatives in ways we don't want to foster.

Attend to Yourself

In their zeal to help their children, parents often fail to nurture themselves. If your nerves are like banjo strings, you're not going to be able to take a deep breath, pause with your first reaction, and analyze your approach. You'll act without thinking, following your innermost agenda.

And yet your child needs a best response for every incident because every incident, no matter how minor it seems to you, is a learning situation. This is the age when kids are packing in every datum they can, then using it to make sense of the world for a lifetime to come.

Humor and irony comprise one avenue. Giving oneself treats is another. These are not bribes for refraining from murder toward the close of day; they are treats, whether deserved or not: A cup of tea drunk at leisure even though a dozen chores call your name. A phone chat with anyone who can string a complete sentence together. A romance novel. A spy thriller. A compact disc of favorite music playing in the background during quiet time with your child.

Giving yourself positive strokes can improve your ability to discipline your child in positive, effective ways.

There are other strategies for encouraging positive discipline as well.

Increasing Your Child's Good Behavior

These suggestions, I trust, you are already doing:

Comment on Positive Behavior and Reward It Judiciously

Bribery has had its place throughout history. Why dump an effective, time-proven method? But please, do it with thought. Reward a child for a job well done but not for *every* job well done. Reward for enthusiasm. And never hesitate to offer a treat "just for being you. I like you!"

Good rewards and treats are not candy. I have more than one friend who never gives sweets to a small child and I have yet to see a small child disadvantaged by this practice. Rewards can be social gestures such as kisses, pats, and hugs (remember the importance of touching to a preschooler), a cracker, a glass of chocolate milk, a story, an invitation to do some special activity. The best rewards cost Mommy and Daddy something: time, in particular.

Another way you can encourage good behavior is by using appropriate consequences.

Allow Consequences

Physics Law Number 1: For each and every action there is a predictable and natural reaction. It's just as true of people.

Consequences are one of the most valuable learning tools you can provide a child. They may be natural or contrived. At this age, the child doesn't make the distinction. A corollary is: Allow the child to fail while it is safe to do so.

"If you don't get done with breakfast quickly, you can't go with Daddy to the store. He has to leave."

The child dawdles. Daddy leaves. The child is heartbroken.

At age one year, this approach would be cruel. In infancy, of course, the child has too little identity to make decisions. But now, on the cusp of Self, the child can handle simple, gentle lessons of cause and effect. How gentle? What sorts of lessons?

The Stakes Must Be Low. The child, just beginning a lifetime of choice, still requires protection from the most drastic of his or her own decisions. In the above example, were Daddy going on vacation instead of to the store, the stakes would be far too high. The consequences would not come close to balancing the behavior in question.

The Cause Must Be Manageable. Can the child reasonably be expected to meet the conditions? A child asked to do something beyond his or her capabilities will learn nothing but frustration and lack of self-confidence.

Let the Child Experience Negative Consequences. It's amazing how difficult this can be on the parents. For example, Ben Schatz's mom would awaken him in the morning for school. Twice. Then she'd nag. Finally he'd get up, and after an inadequate breakfast, barely make it to the corner in time for the bus.

"How far to the school?" I asked.

"Over two miles." Winona obviously guessed my next comment and headed it off. "Much too far to walk."

"He'd only have to walk it once or twice."

Ideally, Winona would call Ben once (well, all right, maybe twice—a sort of snooze alarm). Then Ben would be on his own. You see, the causes and consequences could safely be much steeper for him. A twelve-year-old should be able to comfortably maneuver his way through the morning without adult help.

Winona protested, "He'd be late to school, and he has math first period. I can't let that happen. He's already so far behind as it is." (He was making a high C, not exactly falling on his face in math.)

"Let that be his choice."

Your little one can also make choices and experience the results. Because, unlike Ben, the child is still fully dependent upon you, you can control the consequences and make them appropriate.

For example, should a child touch a hot stove, a burn would be the natural consequence Getting burned on a hot oven door is a lesson. You warned, "That's hot!" The child touched anyway. Bingo.

Pulling a pan of hot soup down on himself or herself would also be natural, but you're not going to let that happen because the child would be severely injured.

Time-out is its own consequence. Impose it when the child refuses to cooperate. Perhaps if the child will not stop throwing things, a favorite toy (presumably one just thrown) is withheld for a time. All these are managed consequences. They are not, strictly speaking, a punishment.

Encourage Positive Consequences. These include the bribe statements you make: "If you can get dressed quickly, we'll have time to play a game together before we go to preschool."

You might call a positive consequence a reward or even a bribe, but it's more accurately a consequence of a good behavior. The behavior and the result are directly linked: Getting dressed quicker leaves time to play.

That's the key to making the lessons of cause and effect work. Tie the consequences to the behavior. Look at the behaviors and logical consequences listed in Figure 7.2; fill in the missing consequences with ones that you think are appropriate.

Increasing appropriate behavior paves the way to introduce new behavior you want to see in your child.

Teach Your Child New Appropriate Behavior

It was an antismoking public service ad on television quite some years ago. A man and his two-year-old boy are washing the car. "Like father, like son," the ad tells us, as if we could not see. The man is obviously encouraging his small son in the task as they ply hose and chamois. Now

BEHAVIOR	LOGICAL CONSEQUENCE
Child resists going to bed.	Child loses chance for a story or other treat with parent before bed. Child spends time before falling asleep alone, no attention from parent.
Child fights with another child over a toy.	Toy is put up. Neither child can play with the toy.
Child plays with her food, throws food at table.	Child is removed from the table. Loses opportunity to eat with parents.
Child behaves at table and sits still during dinner.	Child is given treat appropriate to her interest.
Child runs across the street without looking.	Child is punished. Because punishment is used sparingly it means a great deal.
Child doesn't pick up his or her toys.	_____ _____ _____ _____
Child squirms and talks during church service.	_____ _____ _____ _____
Child plays an entire afternoon without fighting with playmate.	_____ _____ _____ _____

FIGURE 7.2

they are seen seated beneath a tree resting, the job obviously complete. Dad pulls out his cigarettes, lights up, and lays the pack aside. The boy picks up the pack and examines it intently. The voice-over asks, "Like father, like son?"

About the close of this time, as formal school approaches, your child will start mimicking behavior in earnest. Modeling the behavior patterns and acts you want to see in your child is the most powerful positive discipline there is. "Action speaks louder than words" was never more true. For better or worse, your behavior will be mirrored in your child.

But the mirror is cracked. The example you convey is not always the example you want your child to follow. You lose your temper and react in fury; you cool off and realize your blunder. Your sincere apology (yes, indeed, to a preschooler!) patches that mirror and teaches a profound lesson of its own.

Your child, in short, is looking at the whole parent, not the isolated incidents. You will blow it here and flub it there even as it is the whole parent who remains a fine example.

And it is the whole discipline that will be shaped.

Getting It Backward

Put on your raincoat. Now your shirt and a pair of jeans. Now your underwear. Slip your socks on over your shoes. Comb your hair after you've put on a cap.

So often discipline follows the same topsy-turvy progression and achieves about the same success. The parents begin at the last resort, which is to decrease bad behavior, and too often stop there. Instead, they ought to start at the beginning by first avoiding and minimizing inappropriate behavior and then encouraging appropriate behavior, all the while modeling new good behavior.

Heading off problems at the pass is the major premise of effective, positive discipline. It should be a general goal of life.

The child who learns obedience now will develop the self-discipline to obey God later. For the moment, in this third year, you, the parent, are pretty much god. Fortunately for both God and you, that will change with time. Now, though, through your model and guidance, the child will be able to better understand the real Father and do His will.

But there are certain times when it is absolutely crucial that your child be a loud, obnoxious, disrespectful, disobedient brat.

Teaching Deliberate Disobedience

Two unrelated girls aged seven and nine stood on a suburban street corner a little after 8 A.M., waiting for the bus. A man in a bright red minivan pulled to the curb in front of them, opened his car door, and patted the seat. "Hop in. I'll give you a ride and you won't have to wait for the bus."

The seven-year-old stepped forward hesitantly.

The nine-year-old grabbed the little girl's arm and yanked her back. "Run!" Pulling the other child along, she ran down the street toward a mini mart, screaming lustily.

Police followed up on a tip from a customer in the mini mart who heard the screaming, saw the van, and caught most of the license number; they arrested the fellow several hours later. His rap sheet revealed eleven counts of child sexual abuse and attempted abuse.

The older girl had been trained not to obey but to "yell and tell." The training paid off in spades. However, the vast majority of abusers are not strange men prowling the streets, although there certainly are those. The vast majority are friends or relatives, known to the children they abuse.

Cases of child abuse, particularly sexual abuse, do not unfold as isolated incidents. Once a pervert establishes a victim, abuse occurs repeatedly, often over a space of years. Undetected, a perpetrator may literally move from child to child through a family as the children grow by turns to the size preferred. It is therefore essential—*absolutely essential*—that abuse be uncovered as quickly as possible, on or even before the initial incident.

Usually, the only person other than the perpetrator who knows what is going on is the child. The two girls at the bus stop illustrate one reason "yell and tell" is so very important. The other reason is the repetitive nature of perversion.

Is preschool too young to worry about? Sad to say, no, it's not. Infants have been made victims. In fact, two to five is a particularly vulnerable age group. Most children this age do not have the boldness to speak out, and they are utterly at the mercy of any powerful adult or near-adult. How can you protect your child for this danger?

Teach Yell and Tell

I can give you details of several incidents nationwide, one of the most publicized of them in Portland, Oregon, of children who, by screaming persistently, thwarted their own abduction. Your child's response to any overture by an adult who is not in the presence of Mommy or Daddy should be to run away and holler. This behavior will result in a thousand false alarms. So be it.

The child must know that no matter what the person says or promises to do, you make your response loudly, disregarding threats. This is so difficult for a child. The pervert is smooth, quite probably experienced, knowing exactly what bells to ring. "My puppy is lost; please help me find him," or "I'll cut you with my knife if you don't do what I say," or "Your mommy is sick; I'll take you to her." When we hear something like that our suspicions are immediately aroused. Not a small child's.

When the perpetrator is a family friend or a relative, the child's defenses drop to virtual nonexistence. Those defenses will improve as the child grows in maturity, self-confidence, and wisdom. The ground rules below will be valid from now to adulthood.

The Ground Rules

• *My body belongs to me and anything that's covered by a bathing suit is not to be fondled or violated.* No one touches the child in private places except when Mommy or Daddy is present or gives the okay. This gives the green light to the pediatrician with a parent present but not to Uncle X. Remember that this child has not been long out of diapers and is accustomed to being turned bottoms up.

• *I have the right to say no to anyone, even an older sibling or family member, if it doesn't feel right.* Disobedience goes against the grain of children as well as adults. It requires frequent reinforcement.

• *If someone touches me in a secret way, it is not my fault.* Good old global guilt gets in the way here again, augmented by the fact that the perpetrator often tells the child, "It's your fault that . . ." Over and over, the child must hear that he or she is not to blame. Older people must accept their own blame.

• *Never, ever keep secrets, even in the face of threats toward a pet or younger sibling.* No secrets. Period. This is going to steal some of the charm, perhaps, from birthday surprises and other harmless secrets to which the child is privy. Look on the bright side: Preschoolers are terrible birthday-secret keepers anyway.

The ugly truth is that abusers abuse repeatedly by telling the child, "This is our secret. You must never tell anyone."

Here's a rule for the parents in later years:

ALWAYS KNOW WHERE THE CHILD IS GOING AND WITH WHOM.

Teaching the Rules

Telling your child the rules above, even repeating them over and over, will not help should an occasion require their use. At this age the child must learn by doing. No other method will teach. And how do you do that?

Play, "What will you do if . . . ?"

Say, "Pretend I'm a strange man and I say, 'Here, little girl, have an ice cream bar.'" Then demonstrate what the child is to do. Next, lead the child through the motions. Finally, encourage the child to do it independently. Every now and then, repeat the lesson from scratch.

"But I don't want my child to go through life terrified of strangers!" you protest.

And I respond, "Your child is not going through life terrified of streets and swimming pools, yet you do not permit dangerous behavior anywhere near either of them."

Make a game of it. The child sees it as fun; you see it as vital.

Role-playing begins with the second birthday, more or less, and becomes a significant part of your child's learning experience. It will become immensely important for the next few years. You'll have to be more thorough in your guidance with a two-year-old than you would with a four-year-old, directing each move and step.

Signs to Watch For

"I never knew." It's the almost universal response of parents when they learn the horrifying news that their child has been molested. Very frequently there will be no indication whatever that the casual eye would pick up. Still, there are subtleties that *sometimes* appear.

Pay attention if the child suddenly doesn't want to go somewhere in particular or be with someone in particular. This does not necessarily indicate abuse, but it could signal a problem of some sort. Children have a well-developed survival sense. Try not to force compliance if the child feels strongly.

Never force a child to be familiar with an adult if the child doesn't want to. This is not to suggest the adult is an abuser; rather, you do not want to set a pattern that the child is required to go to any person.

Some relatives and friends are simply intimidating to little people. The child cannot articulate why; that does not mean there is no reason. A child might pick up on Aunt Emma's enormous false teeth and be terrified of Aunt Emma. Dear old Aunt Emma wouldn't hurt a soul—she can't even eat corn on the cob—but the child's perceptions triggered wariness. Respect that wariness.

Does the child's urogenital area itch or does the child pick at it excessively? (Children explore casually; that's normal.) Does the child especially try to wash the urogenital area during bath time? Persistent urogenital infections in a child this age are a big red flag.

Does the child use unusual words such as *penis* when there has been no occasion to learn them? Does the child seem surprisingly sophisticated, at least on the surface, about private, personal matters? Should you explore this observation further, avoid asking leading questions. Remember what leading questions are: questions intended to draw out a particular response.

If you observe unsettling signs, watch the child at play alone for a while. A child's play carries deep meanings. Seek professional help if you have reservations, for your peace of mind as much as the child's.

Other Safety Lessons

Fire. A firefighter friend watched the seven nursery-school class members troop through the firehouse bays, clamber over the fire truck, pat the firehouse dog (in this case not a dalmatian but a retired basset hound who did not actually go out on any fires), and admire the firefighters' turnouts all lined up along the wall.

He grimaced. "I'll walk into a burning building gladly, but run a nursery school? You couldn't pay me enough."

To each his own. The children were there to learn about firefighters and to learn fire safety. Each child was taught "drop and roll."

"What do you do if you catch on fire? Drop and roll!" The firefighter demonstrated. The nursery-school teacher repeated the action. The children mimicked it.

"What do you do if you find matches?"
Give them to an adult right away.
"What do you do if you find a lighter?"
Give it to an adult right away.

The children picked up matches and gave them to the teacher. They picked up lighters and gave them to the firefighter. They had a delightful time.

"What do you do if another child is playing with matches?"
You tell an adult.

Fires started by small children playing with matches or lighters are an important cause of injury and death. If you neither smoke nor use a woodstove or fireplace, you may not have matches or lighters in your home at all. That does not preclude your little one from finding them somewhere else.

These basic lessons should properly continue right through grade school. Later they will be augmented by instructions on how to leave a building, how to come to a firefighter (children's first instincts are to hide from them), and how to report a fire.

If your child is not part of a play group or nursery school who would visit the fire station, you may wish to arrange a visit yourself. Fire prevention is a major interest of fire departments, and parents who sincerely want to teach their children safety are generally welcome. Call in advance. A two-year-old is probably too young to appreciate a demonstration by firefighters in air packs, the survival breathing apparatus they wear inside burning buildings. A four-year-old is ready. Your fire department may well have a program or education specialist who can help you at your child's level of interest.

Water. Swimming pools and other bodies of water claim too many small children. You may wish to investigate programs in your area promoting the skill called drown-proofing. Some are pretty good; others are worthless. Whether or not your child takes water lessons, never, ever place your trust in the child's ability to save himself or herself at this age. "Oh, I don't worry about little Junior by the pool. He's drown-proofed." Hardly!

Motor Vehicles. One last safety note: Your child should never ride in a moving vehicle unless he or she is in an appropriate carseat and the seat is properly attached with the seat belt. No exceptions.

"But my kid hates his carseat! He makes so much fuss I let him ride in the back seat when we're just going to the store."

No, no, no! Here is a case where discipline must be constant and absolute. No exceptions. The majority of accidents occur within five miles of home.

No matter how the parents protect and train their children, temporal safety, at best, is chancy. Small children can find so many ways to innocently fall into danger.

Eternal safety is another matter altogether. Preschool is prime time to begin your child down the spiritual road to wholeness and eternal life with God.

8. ENTERING THE SPLENDOR

SPIRITUAL GROWTH

. . . When your children ask in time to come,
saying, "What do these stones mean to you?"
Then you shall answer them . . . And these stones
shall be for a memorial to the children
of Israel forever.

JOSHUA 4:6–7

What is God like?" Marsha Jasper pondered the question a moment as Brian romped across their yard. "I don't know. Sort of like a guy who pays the bills—the Major Bill, of course, the price of sin—but other than that . . ." She shrugged.

"Distant." Jenny answered the same question. "I'd have to say He's probably more distant than some people claim. Not a friend, and sure not warm and snuggly. Just—you know—*God*."

How do you picture God?

Let's try a little quiz. In Exercise 8.1, check as many of the answers as apply to you, going with your gut feeling. There are no right or wrong answers, only interesting ones.

How closely does your picture of God from the viewpoint of childhood parallel your memories of your temporal father? Most people base their first view of God almost wholly on their own earthly fathers. Jesus knew you were going to do that; He compared temporal fathers with the heavenly Father in Matthew 7:9–11.

Your view of God has probably changed somewhat. The differences between your responses to how you pictured God

PARENTAL TRAITS
AND YOUR VIEW OF GOD

1. When I was a child, the way my father treated me (most of the time) was:

   _____ Loving, understanding, and forgiving.

   _____ Judgmental and punitive.

   _____ Distant and/or absent.

   _____ Comfortable and easy to be with.

   _____ A pushover. I could get my way with him most of the time.

   _____ Angry—I was afraid of making him mad.

   _____ Calm, relaxed; he rarely got angry.

   _____ Disappointed. I think my father wished I had turned out differently than I did.

   _____ Approving. My father seemed genuinely proud of my accomplishments, no matter how small they were.

   _____ Fearful and respectful. I was generally in awe of him.

   _____ Unpredictable—I got mixed reactions from him— sometimes loving and understanding, other times angry and punishing. I could never predict how he was going to react.

   _____ I don't really have any strong memories of my father.

   _____ Other: _____

   _____

2. When I was a child, I remember my mother as:

   _____ Strict and unforgiving.

   _____ Judgmental—she always pointed out my mistakes and where I needed to improve.

   _____ Loving and affectionate.

   _____ Forgiving and understanding.

   _____ A good friend; I could talk to her about anything.

   _____ Distant; I felt alienated from her during most of my childhood.

   _____ A sponsor; I could count on my mother to be on my side.

   _____ Distant and/or absent. My mother was gone a great deal during my childhood or she was ill or unavailable.

_____ Unpredictable. I got mixed reactions from her—sometimes loving and understanding, other times angry and punitive.

_____ Stressed. My mother seemed so busy with the house, her job, and/or my brothers and sisters, she rarely had time for me.

_____ Angry and demanding. My mom told me what to do most of the time.

_____ A softie. I could get my way most of the time with my mother.

_____ I don't really remember how she treated me.

_____ Other: _____

_____

3. When I was growing up, I pictured God as:

_____ Angry and frightening.

_____ Distant, big, and unapproachable.

_____ Friendly and approachable.

_____ A friend.

_____ A disciplinarian and taskmaster.

_____ A judge.

_____ Like the Wizard of Oz (before Dorothy and the others found who he really was).

_____ Like a teddy bear.

_____ I don't really remember having a concept of God as a child.

_____ Other: _____

_____

4. But now I'm smart! Now I know God is:

_____ Angry and fearful.

_____ Distant, big, and unapproachable.

_____ Friendly and approachable.

_____ A friend.

_____ A disciplinarian and taskmaster.

_____ A judge.

_____ Like the Wizard of Oz.

_____ Like a teddy bear.

_____ Other: _____

_____

EXERCISE 8.1

during childhood and how you picture Him now should show that. What influences produced the change?

For most people, maturity, studying Scripture, a personal relationship with Jesus Christ, and removal of the earthly parents from the pedestal upon which we held them during childhood all contribute to these changes. Some people need not shift their view appreciably because they had excellent parents who gave them a good model of God. Others have to completely revise their initial picture.

When evangelists work with children in some parts of inner cities, they never refer to God as a Father but as a Friend. All kids know what a friend is; a friend is true blue. In contrast, a father may be someone who beats the kids, abuses Mom, and gets drunk or does crack. God is nothing like the image of a father that many kids harbor.

Do you see from Exercise 8.1 how your relationship with your parents so profoundly shaped your relationship with God, at least initially? Your relationship to your children right now is doing the same thing. What do they see?

Jenny grimaced. "No father at all. That's what rips me; it really does!"

Little Sara would have to draw her initial images from elsewhere. Her grandfather was the man closest to her in life, and he was emotionally distant. Jenny felt emotionally distant from him as well. (Note her description of God in the opening paragraph of this chapter.) Ah, but now Jenny has a lead on Sara's spiritual beginnings: Jenny knows that Sara will feel emotionally distant from God the Father. Jenny can work from that knowledge to help Sara see a fuller, more rounded picture of God. The opposite holds true. By seeing a more complex, closer, grander God, Sara will eventually be able to understand better what a temporal father ought to be like. She will be able to weigh men's characters better than if she had no spiritual grasp of God.

How much of God can a preschooler grasp? At that entry level, so to speak, quite a bit.

Your child's introduction to God will be based upon how you act and react to the child. You are the understudy, standing in for the Star. You can do a good job or a rotten one; either way, you're there. You can't evade the position as stand-in.

It's sobering.

Showing God to a Preschooler

Go through that list of God's attributes again. Which ones do you particularly want your child to see as being God? Those are the ones you should model. That may mean changing some of your basic attitudes about parenting.

God's Attributes

Parents accept certain precepts of theology more or less by rote, not thinking to apply them to the everyday work of raising children. These precepts are all important; they are the ones by which God is raising us, His children.

God's love is not based on action or achievement. It just is.

Ben Schatz was plagued by the knowledge that he had to earn every ounce of his parents' love and affection. Love with a price. And yet, when I asked Edward Schatz about salvation, he expounded at length on Ephesians 2:8, "For by grace you have been saved through faith, and that not of yourselves; it is the gift of God."

Edward and Winona also wanted Ben to have an accurate

view of God. But it never occurred to them that they should be reflecting God in so important a matter—loving Ben simply because he was Ben. Unearned, unconditional love.

God is grace and mercy.

Grace is receiving more blessings than you deserve. Mercy is receiving less punishment than you deserve. How can you offer grace and mercy to a little one who so frequently errs, behaves selfishly, and acts foolishly? You offer it in love, just as God does to you.

Children who would learn of grace and mercy must see it in their parents. And the parents must become aware of the grace and mercy shown to them by others. It amazes me how many parents fail to see these applications in their own lives.

Study your life. What are God's blessings, His grace and mercy, His answers and gifts? As you become aware of them and feel thankful for them, you will lead your child there as well.

God is just, true, upright, righteous . . .

There are many, many strongly moral and ethical people out there who do not know God. They are upright because they believe in uprightness. Goodness. They value honor and integrity for their own sake. Every parent of every child ought to be upright for an infinitely loftier reason: Their small children must see a good God.

Conveying Truth to a Preschooler

Brian scrambled up into Tom's lap with his big Bible picture book, snuggling in with a happy smile. And there they commenced a ritual as old as mankind. A father was about to tell his son a story.

A story.

The Hebrew Scriptures consist almost exclusively of stories. Jesus taught primarily in stories. The great guides of Scripture—the Ten Commandments, the Beatitudes—are jewels set in the matrix of a story.

How ardently does Scripture admonish us, "Tell your children the story . . ."?

In pre-Christian Ireland, where Roman influence was minimal, the wisdom, poetry, sagas, history, genealogies, lore, land records, laws, and edicts—everything was committed to memory. There was no written word. Men would spend twenty years mastering the memorization of a certain body of knowledge. Stories were the means by which all knowledge was passed from generation to generation. The child was expected to hear the story (and be able to repeat it correctly thereafter), ruminate upon it, and derive from it basic truths and philosophies. That system of transfer of knowledge is common to all non-literate societies. Without stories there would be no culture.

Children instinctively understand stories. When a youngster enters my counsel, I cannot give the child a nonfiction answer to his or her problems, so to speak. Children below the age of ten or twelve cannot work with abstracts freely enough to discuss solutions to problems. So I tell stories.

In my stories, a hero or heroine much like my young client encounters a problem similar to my client's. That fictional person solves the problem in an acceptable way. I do not preach. I do not explain. The solution passes from me to the child through the medium of the story, and from it the child understands how to handle his or her problem. Stories really are that powerful.

The story is your avenue to bring God to your child. As Tom read about David and Goliath, Brian was receiving the exciting surface story about a boy with five stones who faced a monster. Below conscious level, Brian perceived also that God stands by His own. That amazing things are possible when God is with you. That no monster, no matter how formidable, is unbeatable. That you have to have faith in yourself as well as in God. That . . .

Surely, you argue, a small child can't pick up all that from a story!

You'd be surprised.

All of this, of course, goes on below a level the child can articulate. A child this small cannot even repeat the story. But the truths come across.

Stories. Bible stories. Lots and lots of stories.

Hiding God's Word in a Child's Heart

Some kids this age are able to memorize like you wouldn't believe. Others cannot memorize at all. For children who like it and are good at it, memorization is a fine way to deeply implant the truths of God. For children who have trouble memorizing, forcing memorization can be hell on earth. You see, some children are not wired for rote memorization. Trying to make them do something that is literally impossible for them not only frustrates them completely and destroys their self-confidence, it severely damages their attitude toward God. That's the last thing you want.

Says my colleague, Dr. Brian Newman, "My Rachel loves to memorize. We make a game of it. There was a spell for a few months there when she didn't seem to enjoy it much, so we backed off. Now she's into it again."

Wisely, he lets his little daughter take the lead, and

his daughter responds by doing what she loves—pleasing Daddy and memorizing. Incidentally, now his son is also doing very well with memorization. Try memorization with your child. But don't force it. Let your child determine whether memorization is effective and if so, how much. At this age, the child isn't trying to get away with something or avoid something because others might laugh. None of the complex reasons older children have for accepting or rejecting spiritual exercises applies now. If your child is wired mentally for memorization, you'll know it.

Teamwork. Moms and dads, working together, have the privilege, responsibility, and blessing of teaching their preschoolers about life . . . and about the God who loves them so much. But what if you are a single parent? I am convinced God has a special place in his heart for single-parent families. In the next chapter we will look at single-parent families and their opportunities to experience God's blessings.

9. SINGLE PARENTS AND OTHERS

ACCEPTING YOUR IMPERFECTION

Children have more need of models than of critics.

JOSEPH JOUBERT

Representing God is frightening enough. But in our society today, we've somehow come to expect parents to be perfect. And that is the source of an immense amount of guilt and worry.

"Perfect parent?" Edward Schatz honestly believed it when he said, "I'd guess I come pretty close."

Beside him his wife snorted. "If you're so perfect, Hot Shot, how come Ben has so many problems?"

It was my delight to be able to point out that Ben didn't really have all that many problems. Then, together we developed strategies for improving Edward and Winona's parenting, the first rule being, as always, to build a relationship.

Jenny and Shauna have a host of additional problems, being single parents, many of which are sheer logistics. Their situation is exacerbated by the fact that they sense perfection is expected of them, and they can't even be half of perfect. The other half is gone.

Perfectionism aside, some difficulties in single parenthood are more easily solvable than others. The success of single parents relies in large part on their attitude.

Dealing with Singleness

Shauna Moore was beginning to feel like a pro. She thought she and Jenny ought to quit their jobs and go into day care full time. They were both single mothers, but they were making it. Sure, it got a little hairy now and then, but they were making it. And look at the experience they were building! With her Afton on one hip and Jenny's Sara on the other and her social economics textbook in hand, she headed for the bathroom.

Sara whined, "I want Mommy."

"Your Mama's gone a-courtin', Honey Child, just like Froggie, and she'll be back by-'n'-by."

Shauna put them down on the postage-stamp-sized bathroom rug. "Strip." She laid aside her book for the moment, signed *undress* to Afton, and started the water running. She'd get her B.S. in business administration, and Jenny could take the child psych courses at the college, and they'd be a rip-roaring concern, making money hand over fist. If Jenny got serious with that Bob Charleston, all the better. He was a teacher; he could be an asset. Day care was the coming thing.

"You brush your teeth first, Sara."

"No!"

"Child, you're gonna be wearing dentures by six if you don't brush your teeth."

"No!"

"Here. You have to take your shirt off. Let me help."

"No!"

Afton hopped to her feet and ran buck naked out the door. Quick as an eel, Sara threw the textbook into the bathwater.

Maybe running a day care facility wasn't such a hot idea after all.

The Kids Who Need Help

People look at the alarming increase in single-parent families in America, never mentioning that the problem is global. These children are the world's future. It is essential that we invest in these families and provide support for them wherever possible. Somehow, supplementing the family life of school-aged kids seems easier (though, frankly, even that rarely happens). At this age, you can invite them out with our own school-aged children to the movies or a ball game. Let them visit, perhaps sleep over.

But the infants, toddlers, and preschoolers need supplemental help as much as older kids—or more. These are the foundational years; this is the formative period. And helping at this time does not seem easy at all.

I have been known to go on at great length about what I consider to be the responsibility of the church toward single parents. I'll not do so here. I will, however, summarize what I see is needed by the children. The relationship between single-parent families and the church is a two-way street.

Single parents must be willing to ask for help

Bob Charleston had his hands more than full with his two small boys. They weren't bad kids; in fact, they were good kids. But small, healthy boys are a handful and a half. His job teaching fifth grade sapped his energy. His kids drained it completely.

His children did not have a significant female to whom they could attach in order to sort out gender identity, except for Aunt Fern. Fern Charleston Brewer had her own family. She included her nephews when she could, but they lived two hundred miles away. The connection was tenuous at best.

If you were to ask Bob why he didn't call upon church members to help him, he would probably say something like, "And let them think I can't handle it? No way. I'll make it."

If you'd get him to voice his innermost feelings, you'd hear, "Pride. Fear that someone might think I'm not adequate. I mean, someone with legal pull to send the kids to my ex-wife. Hey, stranger things have happened, and you can't trust the courts."

Ask Jenny why she did not call more upon the church members to help her; she would probably admit, "Gee, I don't know. I never thought of doing that. Besides, my parents go to that church and . . . you know. How would they feel if I had other church members doing stuff for me instead of them? Mom would turn purple. You know how important appearances are to her."

Myriad reasons prevent single parents from turning to the church. But their children need resources individual church members can provide. The members are, by and large, happy to provide them too. But they have no idea what single parents want and need. Which overtures would be welcome, and which would be misconstrued as an accusation that the single isn't making the cut? What they want to say is, "What do you need? I don't want to offend you. You have to ask me for the help. Guide me."

Single parents able to ask for help from a variety of sources will not be as likely to seek emotional fulfillment in the child.

The job takes nine or ten hours a day. Childcare takes five or six. That's sixteen hours. Adequate rest is seven or eight hours. That's twenty-four. Cooking, laundry, eating, all the nickel-and-dime household stuff that eats your day alive, takes three. That's twenty-seven. An hour to read the paper, catch the news, maybe see a bit of TV, do something for oneself. Now you're up to twenty-eight. By sheer logistics it's obvious that single parents don't get adequate rest, don't get any time for themselves, and their children don't get enough one-on-one time.

Because the children are the only people they see much of in this hectic schedule, single parents are particularly vulnerable to a problem we call emotional incest. It is not by any means incest in the common use of the term. It means that instead of providing the child with emotional energy to grow, the parent draws emotional energy from the child. Evidence of this includes giving the child responsibilities beyond the child's maturity—caring for smaller kids, taking care of himself or herself for several hours a day, preparing meals, becoming a confidant or adviser to the parent ("Tell me, do you think I should go out with So-and-so? What shall I wear tonight?").

The parent who taps into a number of adults, whether closely or casually, is less apt to slide into partial dependence upon a child. Emotional over-involvement is an important phenomenon to watch for, and expanding and intensifying the parent's circle of adult friends and helpers is the solution.

Singles must complete grief for their singleness.

"The loss of a life partner? I never had one." Jenny wagged her head. "What's to grieve?"

Jenny's boyfriend, present at Sara's birth, more or less melted farther and farther into the shadows until he made a de facto exit. Jenny was on her own with few resources. That's what she would grieve. It was appropriate that she grieve the loss of a partner and a partner's help, nearly as if she had been widowed by this boy.

Actual widows and widowers are expected to grieve and are often led by the hand through the process. There are grief workshops for them, support groups, casseroles, and friends. There is closure; the partner is gone. Parents made single in ways other than death do not have that closure. They are not expected to grieve. The attitude seems to be, "You divorced (or refused to marry), didn't you? Your problem is your own fault."

Fat consolation that is!

Single parents must resolve the guilt of denying their child two parents.

Jenny knew that guilt. It plagued her. She dealt with it as best she could. Every time she almost had it under control, it would flare up again.

Shauna, on the other hand, denied hers. "I did what's best in the long run. I have no regrets." Yes, she did have regrets, but she buried them.

Guilt is particularly damaging for two reasons. One has to do with the parent; Shauna was not going to find happiness and resolution in her life until she dug up her guilt and regret and worked through them. The other has to do with the child. Guilt becomes one of those underlying factors that mess up effective discipline.

Jenny recognized her guilt feelings and saw that they might make her overly lenient with Sara—to Sara's detriment. Seeing the problem was the first step in its solution. Shauna didn't see that the same sort of thing was happening to her. She gave Afton much more slack than Afton should have had, and all because of guilt.

Married parents can fall prey to unresolved guilt also, but singles are particularly vulnerable.

The solution? Seek out the company of other single parents who have children your children's age, and talk about the issue of guilt. Their insights will help you, and your insights may well help them.

"I'm not sure I want to talk to total strangers about my problems. Spilling my problems to other parents would make me feel like such a failure," Jenny might say. Bob Charleston would certainly say it.

One of the best ways to begin to deal with guilt is to realize that your feelings, which seem unique to you, are nearly universal. The next step, of course, is to surrender all to Jesus Christ.

Single parents shouldn't try to change facts.

"Someday, before long, Sara is going to ask about her daddy. All her friends have daddies. Why doesn't she? Oh, how I dread that day!"

Jenny and Shauna both faced that problem. Single parents tend to go to extremes in both directions, depending on the circumstances of their singleness. Divorced parents, frequently embittered, will be sure their children know what a lousy human being the ex-spouse was. There are happy exceptions, but that's the general case. You might say the divorced parent is looking at the ex-spouse through smudge-colored glasses.

Widowed parents have a strong tendency to over-eulogize the deceased spouse, minimizing shortcomings and stretching the deceased's candidacy for sainthood. The deification of a lost parent is no more helpful to a child than is the tearing down by an embittered mother or father.

What's the middle ground? Neutrality. It is not the

single parent's place to create or destroy a relationship between the child and the absent parent. The single parent takes care of the single parent's business.

What if Darren, Sara's father, entered Jenny's life at some time in the future, perhaps to claim an interest in Sara? Those are legal issues. They ought be removed from emotional turmoil as much as possible. Only then will the child be spared emotional turmoil.

And keep in mind that the child did not ask for any of this.

The single parent cannot be both parents.
And that's that.

Single parents must see themselves as having something to give back to society.
I visited a church in Albany, New York, that had invited me to give a lecture on childhood development. I was immediately struck by the heterogeny of the congregation. All manner of families and all walks of life were represented. Talk about "the lame and the halt"! People in wheelchairs parked in the aisles. The blind came with their canes, the aged tottered, and the tiny toddled. That heterogeny was matched by an infectious desire for excellence in Christ.

And single parents. They felt welcome here, as did everyone else (as did I!). They were tapping into a rich resource by being part of that church. Just as importantly, they were contributing richly to that resource.

Most of the questions I fielded afterward came from single parents. They knew they needed help, and they asked for it. But they offered help too. They provided me with insights about the "war on the front lines" that I could get in no other way. Those people had something to give.

Single parents can offer much, both to other single parents and to the world at large. When they give as well as receive they become not poor relations in need of charity but part of a powerful dynamic. It's an important difference and a necessary one.

The child comes first.

Yes, the child does come first—but not exclusively to the total neglect of the parent. Jenny was dating again. Apart from the romantic implications, she loved sharing a meal with someone who did not throw Cheerios on the floor. She was serving her own needs. Should her relationship with Bob Charleston develop, she would quite probably be serving Sara's needs as well. But that would be a decision for the future.

Single parents must balance their needs against their child's, and in that field more than all others, single parents tend to feel the guilt of imperfection. In a word, perfection is simply not possible. The parent's hands are too full, the day too short, the needs too diverse. You make do as best you can. It's all you can expect of yourself.

Single parents might take heart in the fact (though I doubt they will) that they are not alone in this pressure toward perfection. Every parent in today's society feels it.

The Myth of the Perfect Parent

Who says every job has to be a fulfilling career? What ever happened to the plain old job that put food on the table and paid the rent? Who says every person can expect to have an ideal life (or sue someone if it isn't), possess ideal children, and escape all significant suffering? Whoever said it, someone believed it. Like Edward and Winona, we've come to think that "the best" means "perfect." Straight A's. No kinks. No errors.

There is only one perfect parent—one perfect anyone. And as they nailed Him to a cross unjustly He did not sue them. He forgave them.

The Christian parent identifies with Jesus Christ without ever hoping personally to become perfect, and yet the goal of the Christian is to ever creep a bit closer toward perfection. It's not a bad philosophy for parenting either.

What is perfect? To never err. But we do. So there is a solution.

Apologize. Ask forgiveness.

What is perfect? To see the ideal answer to every problem and handle the situation in the best interests of the child. We cannot always do this, so there is a solution.

Love.

Love is grace in action, bestowed whether it is earned or not. Forgiveness is mercy in action. Children instinctively understand grace and mercy in their innermost depths, and they respond. Grace and mercy—love and forgiveness—can cover a multitude of imperfections.

Here we go with another story. This is from the royal cycle of Saul, David, and Solomon (many great sagas exist as cycles of three). The story of David, the pivotal member of the cycle, is found in the books of 1 and 2 Samuel and in 1 Chronicles.

The kingmaker, Samuel, anointed Saul of the house of Kish, a Benjamite, king of Israel. But Saul fell pitifully short, not of perfection but of common expectation. So Samuel secretly anointed David, son of Jesse, of the line of Judah, to succeed Saul. Sensing the shift of dynasties, Saul, a textbook psychotic, tried ardently to kill David. Finally, his resources exhausted, David took refuge with Israel's powerful enemies, the Philistines. He attached himself as a mercenary to the Philistine king of Gath.

Now when David went out raiding, he would strike frontier clans allied with the Philistines, then return to Gath and tell the king he was hitting Israeli border settlements. To protect his dirty secret, he killed every man and woman in the villages, lest they carry the truth to Gath. Hundreds of innocents died.

David paid for his first wife, Michal, with the foreskins of two hundred Philistines. When eventually he took the crown, he was responsible for thousands more deaths as chief of the armies. And then he spotted Bathsheba. You know that story of lust and deception. Bathsheba's husband, Uriah, died in the heat of battle, his death engineered by David from behind the lines.

God cursed David for one death only. Out of the hundreds and hundreds of deaths he caused, at least some of them totally innocent and undeserving of destruction, one death. Uriah's. And yet, even as He cursed, God forgave.

I am a great believer in the ancient practice of studying the stories for the truths they convey, perhaps because I use the method of storytelling myself. The cycle of David contains many, many profundities beneath the surface tale.

During the latter days of David's exile from Saul, that year he spent at Gath, he found himself, to quote the old saying, between a rock and a hard place. Killing innocents was not right—no one suggests it's okay—but God let him off the hook. In fact, God blessed his efforts. That's mercy where it counts—when the sin is deliberate but there's not much choice in the matter.

In church we pray for small mercies, and I am not belittling that in the least. But it does not begin to tap the width and depth of God's mercy. Nowhere near.

David's hardened attitude in the matter of Uriah was the greater sin in the Bathsheba incident, as Nathan so skillfully pointed out. That attitude of the heart was punished. Mercy, though, covered an untold multitude of other errors.

Now I apply that to myself as a parent. I will make mistakes from time to time, and I will be forced into compromising circumstances where I must make the best of a bad situation. I may not do real well at that. So I will keep my eyes on God, on Jesus Christ, and do the best I can according to His words and example. I will love and forgive my child. Grace and mercy. I will ask (but not demand) love and forgiveness of my child. I will try to show Jesus to my son through me.

That's not egotism. That's survival.

Free Flight

In this book I have tried to explain the world from your small child's point of view and help you see what the child's needs are at an emotional and psychological level. When those two classes of needs are well met, nearly everything else falls into place. My view of the preschooler is educated but not perfect. Your parenting is inspired but not perfect. Your child is eager and open but not perfect. Thanks to God for His grace and mercy, none of us has to be perfect. It's covered.

That leaves us free to embark on a saga of our own as

intriguing as any king's. We are free to raise up a new soul unto the Lord, not as a burden and duty but as an adventure. From total dependence to independence with attachment, a new and fully rounded person will rise up beside you, take wing, and fly. Don't forget to let go.

Grace and mercy, both yours and the Lord's, need an avenue of expression, and that avenue is your relationships. One will be with your child, the other with God. Let love flow freely in both directions.

God bless your royal adventure!

ABOUT THE AUTHOR

Paul Warren, M.D., is a behavioral pediatrician and adolescent medicine specialist. He serves as medical director of the Child and Adolescent Division and the Adolescent Day Program of the Minirth Meier New Life Clinic in Richardson, Texas and also has an active outpatient practice. He also is a professional associate with the Center for Marriage and Family Intimacy based in Austin, Texas.

Dr. Warren received his M.D. degree from the University of Oklahoma Medical School. He completed his internship and residency at Children's Medical Center in Dallas, Texas where he also served as chief resident. He did a fellowship in behavioral pediatrics and adolescent medicine at the University of Texas Southwestern Medical School and Children's Medical Center in Dallas.

An expert in child and adolescent issues, Dr. Warren is a popular seminar speaker who addresses audiences nationwide and is a regular guest on the Minirth Meier New Life Clinic radio program. His other books include *Kids Who Carry Our Pain*, *The Father Book*, and *Things That Go Bump in the Night*.

Dr. Warren and his wife Vicky have a son, Matthew.